The Wonder of Growing

by DR. ESTHER P. EDWARDS

THE FIRST THREE YEARS OF LIFE—
A PARENT GUIDE TO EARLY LEARNING

Sears | GOLDEN WONDER OF GROWING PROGRAM

Book Design by Jos. Trautwein

Photographs by Martin Bough
    Selected photographs by Erika and
    Container Corporation of America

Edited by Vana Earle

library of congress catalog card number: 73-162325

Contents

4

Program Author
DR. ESTHER P. EDWARDS
Associate Professor
Eliot-Pearson Department of Child Study
Tufts University

Associates

Sylvia Feinburg
Instructor and Director
of Student Teaching
Eliot-Pearson Department of Child Study
Tufts University

Frances Ackerly
Educational Coordinator
Family Day Care
Cambridge-Somerville
Catholic Charities, Massachusetts

Under the editorial direction of Vivian Bennett

Board of Advisors

Dr. Bettye Caldwell
Professor of Elementary Education
Director, Center for Early Development
and Education, University of Arkansas

Mary Ann Scarlette
Coordinator
Early Childhood and Elementary Education
Bennett College, Greensboro, North Carolina

Dr. Peter Gardetto
Pediatrician
Kurten Medical Group, Racine, Wisconsin

Dr. Philip Jackson
Professor of Education and Human Development
University of Chicago

Dr. Evelyn Goodenough Pitcher
Professor and Chairman
Eliot-Pearson Department of Child Study
Tufts University
Medford, Massachusetts

Cyrus Porter
Director, Product Development
Western Publishing Company

Dear Reader:

In the past several years, teachers, psychologists, and child development specialists have become vitally interested in a new point of view about the value of experience in early childhood. No longer do they believe that a baby's intelligence is fixed at birth. While realizing that the child's heredity plays an important part in his or her growth, they now know that it is not everything. Unless the child is given enriching experience even the greatest potential intelligence fails to develop as it should.

Through testing and examining babies and young children, psychologists have developed theories to help them understand what takes place as a baby grows. They know that the brain approximately doubles in size during the first two years of life. Not that new cells are made but those existing at birth become connected in more and more intricate ways. In time the baby's brain becomes a complex network of multiple cells along which travel the electrical impulses that trigger all activity. Scientists believe that these connections develop best when the child is exposed to interesting experiences—experiences which provide a sense of satisfaction and reward, and most important, experiences which are appropriate for the child's level and stage of growth. In response to experiences of this kind, the child can actively build an inner system which allows him to perceive clearly and to think and understand, to solve problems and create imaginatively.

Such experiences can be provided through the medium of playthings—toys which are designed to feed major areas of active development characteristic of each stage in a baby's life. The child must be ready for the toy to get the most from it. A good toy allows the child to discover, build and test out skills and concepts at his own speed without frustration. A good toy is challenging, fascinating enough to engage the child's attention during moments of concentration. A toy is particularly productive if it can be used in different ways as the child grows.

Toys alone cannot provide all that is needed for growth. But given a loving and healthy climate for development, the child's mental and physical progress will be stimulated by the content of well chosen playthings.

With loving and caring in mind, this book is dedicated to the parent—the child's first teacher. It's purpose is to help you better understand your child —his or her development, unique personal interests, strengths and needs—and to truly enjoy the wonder of growing you see before you.

Esther P. Edwards

INTRODUCTION

A child is born. A new being has appeared in the
world. For a moment we catch our breath at the
thought of the intricate unfolding of this child's life
for years and years into the future.

At birth infants are at once new and ancient expressing through their built-in reflexes trends of
development that have shaped the human race over
millions of years. These hereditary capacities permit
life to be carried on until infants can begin to direct
their own actions. They grasp, they suck, they respond to light, to sound, to pressure, to heat and
cold. They come equipped with the muscular reactions that allow movement, breathing, absorption
of water and food. Even though as yet they feel no
conscious recognition of the world about them, they
are beginning to gain familiarity with their environment.

Though the newborn baby is a marvel of com-
plexity-muscles, bones, blood vessels, organs, all related one with another in a functioning system, it is

still the most incomplete, the most dependent of all young creatures. The longest infancy and childhood in the animal world lies ahead. What this new human being will be is not wholly determined. It's heredity sets limits, offers avenues.

But potentials must be realized! The sensitized photographic plate bears an invisible image. Put it in a chemical bath and the image, the picture, will appear perfectly, or imperfectly, depending on many factors. So, too, with the baby and the experiences it meets. Only as good things happen, in good time—as they can be used—do the infant's potential abilities become fact.

Of all the circumstances the baby encounters, parental care and love are the most important. Parents provide the solid base which allows the child to feel safe enough—good enough—to reach out and accept the world, its challenges, frustrations and rewards. The loved child who finds the most important beings in his experience responding sensitively, meeting his needs, providing "food" for his developing abilities truly has a head start.

Offering this care is the most important task anyone can do. It is the one on which all others rest. Each child born renews humanity, continues mankind. Without this new growing child, what would be the value of skyscrapers, vitamin pills, new cars, art museums full of treasures, supermarkets full of produce? Remember, every day during a child's early years has its own significance.

Our mothers were told, "Keep the baby warm, fed, clean and dry, treat it with kindly affection—otherwise leave it alone." They thought children would unfold like the leaves of a tree by means of some kind of built-in blueprint activated by the normal maturation of the body. Now we know a child needs more: a child needs mental stimulation right from the very start. What kind of stimulation? How should it occur? These are the basic questions we asked when we started a three year research and development project which became The Sears-Golden Wonder of Growing Program.

During the first year of the project all the research data in the field were compiled to provide an overview of child growth during the first three years of life. Highlighted were: changes in physiological development, sensory and motor coordination, social and emotional growth, and cognitive and symbolic processes. The result is a distillation of all that is known today. This serves as the backbone of the total program.

The next two years involved a continuing dialogue between many creative people—specialists in early learning, teachers, psychologists, designers, artists, writers and so on. The result was a direct translation of research data into playthings. From over one hundred designs which were created and subjected to critical review, the final twenty-five were developed.

As the program developed, the importance of parent participation became increasingly evident. In talking with mothers, we learned that not only were they interested in learning how to use the toys more effectively, they wanted to find out about growth in a broader context as well. And so this book came into being. Just as the sequence of playthings is the program for the child, this book is the program for parents who are interested in learning about how the child learns.

The book is organized for quick reference or in-depth use. There are three main chapters: *The First Year, The Second Year, and The Third Year.* Each chapter deals with the particular time period on several levels. The overview of each year describes the processes of growth in general terms: how the infant, then the baby, then the child copes with the world in constantly expanding ways as abilities grow.

The second section of each chapter is called *Discovering the World Through Toys.* This section deals with the program specifically: what we expect at a particular time of development; what the toys will do; and how you, the parent, can be more effective. This section has three parts.

Growth Objectives offers the reader a compact but comprehensive study of typical aspects of mental, physical and emotional advancement for each three month period—months 1 to 3, 3 to 6, 6 to 9 and so on. The parent who is immediately interested in knowing what pertains to a particular age can find it in here.

The Right Toy at the Right Time, in photographs
and words, gives a detailed description of the playthings to be introduced during each three month in-
terval. The program consists of twenty-five playthings organized in a sequence of twelve series starting from birth. Some series contain as many as four
toys, while others contain one depending on the
needs of the child and the play possibilities inherent
in the toys. Look for this subtitle when you are interested in learning the purposes and uses of the playthings as they apply to your child. It is a helpful
reference when you want to learn about the toys
planned for the months ahead.

The Part You Play suggests ways in which the toys,
books, and activities can be introduced, and how you
can participate so as to become more deeply a part
of your child's growth. Here are hints on using the
playthings in different ways and specific do's and
don'ts: when to join your child in play, or when to
enjoy just by watching. For your child's behavior
has meaning, and you can learn to interpret and
understand his steps toward learning.

This book, therefore, can be used in several ways.
It is enjoyable and instructive to read through from
the first page to the last. It describes the marvelous
journey from birth to age three. Before you introduce your child to a particular series of playthings,
however, you may want to turn to those pages that
deal with children the age of your own.

Good Reading!

THE 1ST YEAR

HERE IS YOUR BABY, warm in his crib, kicking his legs, blowing a milky bubble, yawning and falling asleep—an individual in the making—full of unknown possibilities. How does it all begin?

WHAT DOES YOUR BABY KNOW? At birth, nothing at all: no words, no mental images, no ability to think as an adult thinks, no knowledge of the surrounding world, nor any knowledge of existing as a self. No knowledge at all. This was where we all started. We all had to find out about ourselves—even that we existed—and about the world at one and the same time. For each discovery is part of the other. All this lies ahead of the newborn child.

WHAT DOES YOUR BABY FEEL? Body states: hunger, satisfaction, warmth, cold, pressure, the motion of limbs, torso, and head. There are no labels to attach to these feelings as yet and no way of remembering from moment to moment (for we remember through images and words) but with quite marvelous speed the infant begins to sense some things as familiar.

HOW DOES YOUR BABY LEARN? When picked up to be fed for the first time lips fasten on the nipple from which the milk flows with some help, or only by accident. But soon he goes directly to it. In a purely physical way the baby senses the shape and texture which provide satisfaction.

The child is hungry and fussing in the crib and as his mother leans down to pick him up he calms down and relaxes. "He recognizes me already," she says with delight. Not quite so; what a child recognizes now (at a month or two months) is a situation. Somehow, deep inside its body, through its muscles, nerves and organs comes a feeling of the known, the familiar. It is as if the body were saying, "This has happened before, and it means comfort soon." This is the way the child learns to feel at home in its small world.

THE SUCKING REFLEX is an inherited gift, already present in the newborn baby's repertoire of skills. Yet even so, he learns very soon to suck more effectively, with less wasted motion. Soon the baby is sucking parts of his own body from which food does not flow: fingers, thumbs, anything that reaches the mouth. "Oh dear," says his mother. But she should not be concerned. This is a passing phase. Through use of the inherited reflex of sucking the baby learns about self and world.

But supposing these reflexes, these hereditary functions are not stimulated, not encouraged to develop, what then? Then they not only do not develop, but soon the very possibility of using them becomes lost. Keep a normal, sighted baby in a totally dark room too long—for months—and the power to see is lost. The power to control the eyes, to respond to light, vanishes. To be kept, the reflexes must be used.

But give the baby the experiences that relate to the inborn capacities of the reflex system, and these develop and in time connect in complex ways which are the basis for all that will be learned later on.

WHAT DOES YOUR BABY SEE? We used to be told that it took weeks for the sense organs to reach any degree of usefulness. We know now that this is not so. Infants like lively patterns more than solid colors, even if the two are equally bright. They show this by paying much more attention to the pattern than the solid— which clearly they could not do unless they could see it in the first place! There seems to be a human interest in variety present even from the very beginning.

THE SENSES ARE WORKING, and well, from the first days. Yet babies cannot use all the information which comes from the world about them. Unlike adults, though their senses pick up the clues that add up to form, direction, location, weight, and so on, these measures of the world have no meaning as yet. Your child reacts to light. But it is only a passing show, delightful for its own sake, but conveying absolutely no information.

Why is this? What does it mean? It means that every human being, every one—your child, all children—must truly build their own worlds from scratch. The newborn baby has not yet had a chance to do this. Signals are received through the senses, but the signals do not have meaning. Adults are aware of a jumble of shapes, colors, sounds, textures, and so on. But we put these together and our minds comprehend a room, a street, a landscape, a world. A baby is aware of the same jumble. But much learning must go on before he can put it together and know what it means.

THE GREAT TASK OF MIND is sorting out the jumble. It is the task upon which everything that happens in the following years will rest. This is what your child is doing lying in the crib or cuddled in your arms. You provide the warm loving acceptance which allows this to happen. But all babies must learn for themselves what every signal means before they can become fully developed human beings.

HOW CAN YOU HELP your child in this major task? Of all the things in the world the human face is best—the pattern of your face is your child's greatest delight. It is a pattern to which he is already set to react. But that pattern is far more interesting because it changes: it moves; it wiggles; the eyes open and close. From the round mouth comes interesting noises. This face appears at the important times of his life: when he wants to be fed, when he is wet and uncomfortable, when he is too hot or too cold, when something excites him. It does something about the way he feels—generally, it makes him feel better. If this face and the person attached to it show warmth, acceptance, support and love, the infant knows this and relaxes and grows—physically, emotionally, intellectually and socially.

BEYOND BASIC NEEDS, you can give him interesting things to look at, to listen to, to feel, smell, taste, and touch—something bright placed where he can see it easily, a window to look through (no sun directly in his eyes, though), something that moves; the possibilities are endless. After the first couple of months, he can usually follow things that move and can begin to focus his eyes to near and far. Vision is your baby's first teacher. Watch him. He is intense in his looking. Often something

newly seen will seem to freeze him. He lies completely
still, all his energy going into his seeing—then he moves;
his arms and legs wave; he makes cooing sounds or
chuckles; his whole body responds with a burst of energy.

AS THE MONTHS PASS—the third, fourth and fifth
months—your baby is busy fitting together sense impres-
sions. In the beginning, there were many separate
worlds, one for each sense. A world of what it saw,
a world of what it heard, a world of taste and feel and
smell. Your baby could hear a sound, without any
urge to try and see what made it. So far as it was aware,
nothing made it and it implied nothing out there. But
now these different worlds begin to overlap. Now the
baby listens intently to the jingling of its rattle and
tries to see the sound. What the baby sees is the color,
shape, and form of the rattle. And now, perhaps one
of its hands or a foot grazes it by chance. Something
can be felt. After many chance encounters, there is
a dawning realization that a sense impression is a clue to
something—that *something* is there—an object that can
be felt, or heard, or seen, and usually all of these at once.
As the senses come together, the world begins to be
thought of as having three dimensions—the world becomes real!

JUDGMENT BEGINS. Now your baby grasps not
just because grasping is possible but for a purpose. It
looks in order to see, listens in order to hear—*something*.
Now your baby begins to have wishes and goals. It can,
at last, begin a few simple acts on its own. The child,
at this stage, is no longer a puppet, passive, moved
only by the actions of the outside world or inner signals
which cannot be resisted. Now your child has begun to
become a being with a will of its own. It begins to be

aware of cause and effect (I kick, and the colored balls jangle so I like that, so I'll kick again). And your child is also becoming aware of time, for there can be no realization of *this* causing *that* without the passage of time. Judgment is in operation as it chooses something, however simple, as a goal of action. Here is where individuality and intelligence can both be said to have entered into the picture. Before this the child was acting from instinct. Now the child has become, in truth, a person with a mind of its own.

PHYSICAL CONTROL INCREASES. All this time the child has been gaining strength and control over its body. It has become able to lift its head, to turn over, to control hands and then feet, to begin to pull up to a sitting position. By eight months some babies (generally light, wiry children) are pulling themselves up and taking first steps, though other perfectly normal, strong babies will not walk till much later.

NOW FINGERS HELP. The mouth has been a prime source of information about the world. The child has gone through the stage of simply plopping everything it grasps instantly into the mouth. Now he positions things first. For instance, the part of the teether that lends itself best to being chewed will go directly into the mouth. To be able to do this simple act of placement, a child must have come to understand that objects are real and that he can handle them according to some plans he has made in his mind: a major advance over the hit or miss ways of earlier behavior. Interesting things to put in the mouth and chew have been of great value in this development, but now the important part of the body used for learning about the world by feeling, manipulating, becomes the fingers. The child has learned how to control his hand by looking at it. Now he becomes so sure of where it is and what it can do, that he no longer needs to look at it as it moves and holds. Hands and fingers send into the system new kinds of knowledge about the world: how weight shifts when you move an object from here to there and what that feels like; and information about textures, shapes, sizes, temperatures of objects.

YOUR BABY'S INTERNAL TEMPO should be respected. Many eight-month olds are scooting about: hitching along on their stomachs, creeping, crawling, sometimes very rapidly. Because they can move around, the segment of the world they come into contact with is larger and their knowledge of who and where they are increases rapidly. But remember, your baby is an individual. Some children talk early, some children walk early—and some babies, now grown into very bright adults, didn't do either. Enjoy your baby for the wonder that he or she is—as is.

YOUR BABY IS ON THE MOVE. The one-year-old child has changed from a helpless, squalling infant to a true individual who knows the world as a real place, and himself as being in it. Many capacities have begun to develop. In every area, your child has come a long way in three hundred and sixty-five days.

Discovering the World through Toys

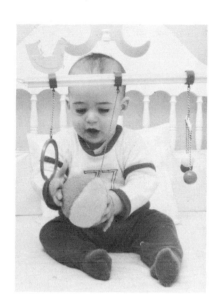

Growth Objectives: MONTHS 1 to 3

The newborn infant arrives equipped with the reflexes needed to sustain life: it breathes, sucks, cries when uncomfortable, grasps at an object that brushes its palm. It is, in every way, a minimum package, but from the moment of birth this new being is working towards improving these life-sustaining reflexes. Of all of these, the ability to see is the most significant, the one that starts the learning process.

We know now, that at birth, babies can tell light from darkness and, amazingly, within only four days they are able to see patterns of one-eighth inch stripes at a distance of ten inches, and there is already a preference for complex over simple designs. Research suggests, that even at this early age, the infant can make comparisons of different patterns.

During this stage of its existence, the infant will stare at its own hand, or at an object placed within its range of vision. But soon it will attempt to follow a moving object with its eyes and later will make the effort to turn its head in that direction.

Other things are happening, too. During this first three month period, the baby may smile at the sight of a human face and towards the end of this time begins to put together seeing and hearing. The baby hears something and looks in that direction—mother's face when she speaks, for instance.

After a while the baby who has been listening to sounds of its own making, tries to imitate these same sounds. While this is going on the baby also begins to recognize situations as having occurred before. He begins to expect the familiar. There is a start towards coordination of grasping and sucking reflexes. Anything that is grasped goes immediately to the mouth.

In three short months, given the stimulation it needs, the baby looks and really sees; hears and tries to imitate; reaches out to grasp seen objects; and makes a variety of sounds to show pleasure as well as discomfort. It has come a long, long way!

Toys that are developed in keeping with these facts of growth are important educational aids that stimulate the processes of nature. At this age, toys should offer a visual message—see what an interesting place the world is.

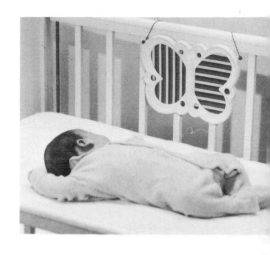

The Right Toy At The Right Time: SERIES 1

CRIB PLAQUE ™

This first toy provides simple visual stimulation during brief waking periods. A delightful, colorful butterfly plaque hangs inside the crib within the infant's range of vision. A series of cards (bulls-eyes, stripes, checker-boards and a solid color) are inserted into the plaque so that they are framed by the wings of the butterfly. Changed periodically, these cards provide a continually interesting focus for baby's attention.

The cards have been designed in such a way that one wing is always stronger and more vibrant than the other. This is compelling to the infant and encourages comparison. Eyes shift back and forth strengthening the muscles of vision, but most important, the baby is challenged to move towards true "thinking."

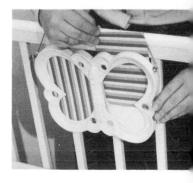

CRIB MOBILE _{TM}

The sun, moon and stars float above the baby's head moving, shifting, providing interesting variations in form and color, (yellow crosses over blue, and mysteriously, green appears). The stars hang at varying distances from the child in the crib, move slowly, giving a sense of objects in a three dimensional space. The child can derive a sense of near and far. Eye muscles strengthen as eyes try to follow the movement and concentration is demanded, too. Instead of the blankness of a white ceiling, there is the interest of a constantly altering pattern which repeats itself often enough to be familiar, friendly—learnable. At the time when the eyes begin to follow moving objects within the visual field, the *Crib Mobile* helps the baby to gain control, focus, and exercises the developing power of visual pursuit.

The Part You Play: SERIES *1*

Place the *Crib Plaque,* on the crib where your child can see it at eye level. A built-in reflex called the tonic neck reflex will cause the baby's head to turn toward one side or the other. Check to be sure that the toy is in view when this occurs. Some babies prefer to lie on their stomachs. In these cases it may be better to place the toy at the head rather than the sides of the crib.

Remember, your baby is only awake for short periods, often awakening because of hunger or other discomforts. Do not expect the toy to soothe your baby and quiet fretfulness. It may, indeed, do so for a brief spell, but during this first month of life inner urgencies compete with the stimulation of the outside world.

The function of the toy is to be constantly in view, interesting and familiar when the baby's interest is catchable. By simply being there, it will increase the baby's desire to look more and more and grow more and more aware of things outside himself.

The cards of patterns and colors found to be most fascinating to infants should be changed periodically when the baby's interest wanes. In this way, new and interesting combinations will awaken the baby's interest in comparison. You will be amazed to see how your child is discriminating between very similar patterns. Slight shifts in eye movement will be your clue.

The *Crib Mobile* serves its maximum purpose when the baby can follow motion with the eyes. Hang this toy over the crib where it can be looked at with ease as the baby lies on its back, not overhead, but slightly in front, and where it does not interfere with your actions when you are handling the baby.

In time, your baby will gaze intently at the *Crib Mobile* following the motion and color patterns. There is just enough to look at. It is varied enough to keep the baby interested. The stars move near and far and the sun and moon glide slowly in their arcs. Sounds and excited body motions or moments of quiet concentration are clues to baby's satisfaction in looking. This will happen when the baby is ready to observe motion.

Growth Objectives: MONTHS 3 to 6

Your baby's progress during this period will be easier to see and so, perhaps, more exciting. It is a time when the entire household will find itself rushing to the cribside because someone calls, "Come here quickly, Peggy has turned herself over!" or, "Look, look! Tony is holding his head up all by himself" or, "Oh my! sitting up without my holding!" The child is at the beginning of putting together separate worlds: the world of seeing, the world of touching, the world of hearing.

The baby moves more freely from side to side; can hold its head erect for a moment; can reach and push with an open hand, and will soon be able to turn over. Now the bottle is held, the hands can join over the body and play—finger touching finger. Control has been gained over hands: they can open and close, the index finger is used by itself, to touch some desired object.

The baby likes to sit up supported by an arm or a pillow, often lifts the head and even tries to lift the body. It has learned to balance its head on neck and shoulders and is moving towards being able to balance the body.

Toward the end of this time span the baby will be able to sit for a short time without support. Some babies begin to pull themselves up, though this only results in plunking down again.

The baby will grasp a hanging object, and can hold two objects at one time, one in each hand—will position an object before sucking it—that is, will place the most interesting part of the object in the mouth. Until now, the baby has sucked for the pleasure alone. At this point this reflex becomes a way of learning about objects.

There is a difference now in the sounds the baby makes: some have meaning to the mother. The baby is aware of these sounds and repeats those it finds pleasant. At first it is trial and error, a particular sound is repeated by accident, but recognition is there, also. Later during this period the sounds made are often responses to familiar faces, toys, and other objects. Jimmy or Janie or Marie may recognize the sound of their own names. The baby likes the company of others, in particular, familiar persons.

There is a steady shift of interest from the usual, the known, towards the less usual, the less known. The child learns fastest at the point where what it observes is just a little strange and new, yet not completely unknown.

Scientific research has shown that major visual development has taken place in this six month period. The familiar sight of a baby beginning to fret or cry when an unfamiliar person looks into the crib or carriage shows that, at this age, the child knows what the members of the family look like.

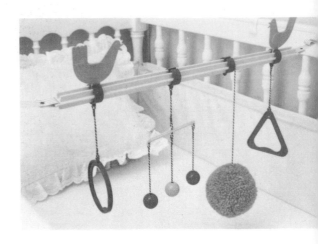

The Right Toy At The Right Time: SERIES 2

COORDINATOR CRIB GYM ™

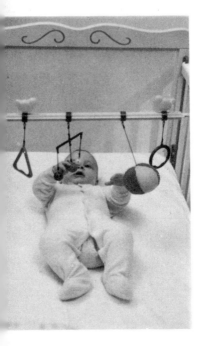

The *Coordinator Crib Gym* is designed to meet many needs at this time in the child's life. The large plush ball and the smaller, brightly colored balls attract the child's gaze. An accidental movement of hand or foot will set the objects swinging. This is something exciting—something marvelous! After a bit, hands and feet connect more regularly with their target. The *Gym* motivates the child to exercise. And, as time goes on, the child gains greater control. As muscles mature, the child discovers the delightful possibilities of lifting the head and torso. Hand-holds help the raising process and increase physical strength.

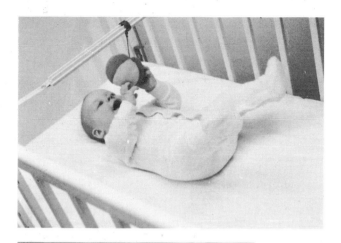

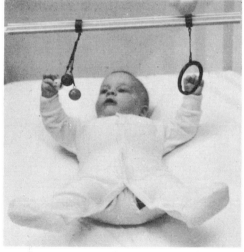

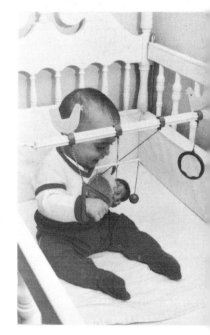

And all the while, there is the stimulation of seeing shapes and colors, of hearing a tinkling sound when the balls are kicked, of touching and grasping things which send new information about hardness, softness, and texture—to be wondered about by the active brain.

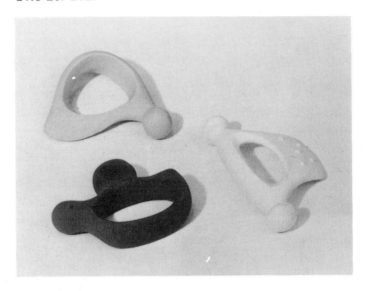

TENDER TEETHERS ™

Tender Teethers are shapes to suck, to feel with the tongue and gums and to push against to relieve the pain of teething. These toys are designed for the time in the baby's life when his sensitive mouth gives him vivid input about the world. They are planned to fit the baby's hand, as well, so

that he can hold them and place them in his mouth without losing them. This is a period when coordination between oral activity and grasping is in a beginning stage of development. Smooth and knobbed or ridged sections of these soft teethers offer texture interest. Each teether has been designed to encourage exploration in a variety of ways. And safety features have been incorporated into their free-form designs.

TOUCH MUCH

Touch Much, a soft, safe, wipe-it clean rattle, supplies the child's needs at an important developmental point when the mouth ceases to be the prime source of discovery—when the hands take over. The toy is large enough for the child to gain a sense of bulk and weight, yet not too heavy for muscular capability or

control. A handle allows for grasping and holding; a noise-maker inside the toy rattles, louder or faster, controlled by the hand waving the toy. The cool, satiny, firm-to-the-touch plastic handle contrasts in temperature and texture with the rough towelling and the raised, smooth weaves of the different brightly colored fabrics that cover the soft cone. It focuses the child's attention on the different ways his world feels.

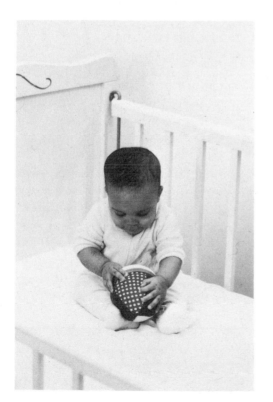

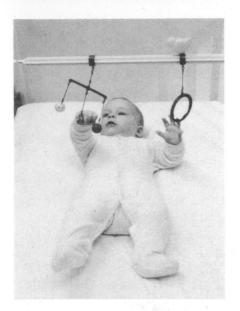

The Part You Play: SERIES 2

Position the *Coordinator Crib Gym* so that your child can move the balls with hands and feet. Show that the balls move by swinging them gently yourself when you have the child's attention. Smile—the pleasure in your face is a clue. If, the first, second or even third time, no interest is shown, leave the *Coordinator Crib Gym* in place and repeat the process of swinging the balls every so often. The baby will take over when ready to do so.

The *Coordinator Crib Gym* is adaptable to the play-pen. When it becomes a familiar, favorite toy use it to make your child feel at home in a new and unfamiliar situation. It may, for instance, be useful to bring it along on an auto trip and tie it to the car-bed or wherever it is within the child's reach.

The Gym is constructed for ease of handling and cleaning. Elements can be shifted, pushed to the sides or removed for washing. You may find that, at first, your baby is only interested in the large plush ball—in that case slide the small plastic balls, triangle and circle hand-holds to the side, or remove them—to add, one at a time, when interest in a new aspect of this toy can be awakened.

Offer a *teether* to the baby. Watch. See how quickly your baby gets the idea. In almost no time at all the most delectable part of the teether will get to the mouth! Does he approach each teether differently? Does he have a favorite?

The *Touch Much* should not be introduced before the child is sitting up alone. Wave the *Touch Much* and make it rattle, then place it in the crib near the child when he is awake and not fussing.

The important thing when introducing any toy is to show the pleasure it evokes. The second most important thing is to allow your child to decide when to discover its appeal. Enjoy the various ways your child explores the toy—touching, squeezing, shaking, rolling or holding.

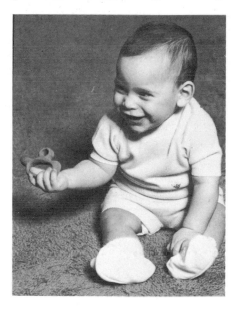

Growth Objectives: MONTHS *6 to 9*

Now the baby sits unsupported and can stand with help. This is a period of great progress from beginning to end. In a very short time the baby may raise itself to a sitting position. A very few children are starting to pull themselves up. As their coordination improves they will be able to stand wth the support of the playpen corner.

Because the child is emerging as an individual, there is great variety of attainment. The baby is beginning to practice picking up objects with its fingers. Wrist motion is somewhat under control. And most of all, the child now has the built-in knowledge of where its hand is. Now objects can be grasped without visual direction. As this period spins itself out, the thumb and forefinger are used and the hand tilts before grasping, showing that there is the expectation of touching something solid. Cause and effect behavior is more conscious and a sense of time is apparent. The child will grasp an object immediately. But if an object is held in each hand and a third is offered, the baby puts down one of the objects before grasping the other. And now things are used as tools (a string, a stick, as well as a hand or foot) in order to obtain the desired object.

There is a growing awareness of the permanence of things. A child will learn during this period to reach for a toy outside the crib even if only a part of it can be seen as a visual cue. Now the eyes follow a rapidly moving object and try to look after it as it disappears.

Babies, in this age group, will smile at their own images in the mirror and may pat the image. They have learned to enjoy the presence of other children. The game peek-a-boo is a delightful possibility because the child has become sensitive to familiar people and is exploring the laws of appearance and disappearance. There is an expectation of reappearance, but not enough certainty to make it a dull game. Something that disappears will reappear, maybe!

Some children may be saying "da-da" or "ma-ma," others will be imitating sounds not of their own making. And there seems to be an awakening interest in sounds not just as sound, but as meaning—as words.

This is the beginning of the time when the child tries to act upon its environment, not merely respond to stimulus. The world is growing larger, more three-dimensional. The child is beginning to learn some of the world's regularities and is in fact acting with true intelligence.

The Right Toy At The Right Time: SERIES 3

LOLLISPOON ™

Lollispoon is a problem-solving and rattle teether toy that provides the kind of satisfying surprise that will reinforce the child's growing awareness of object permanence. The inner core is chewable and has ends varied in shape and texture and weight. It slides back and forth when tipped, hiding one end from view

—appearing and disappearing in a way which is mystifying, at first. Gravity makes it work, an unknown fact to the child, who nerevtheless gradually learns to control it. Here is a toy that offers the experience of now-you-see-it-now-you-don't and allows the child to repeat the experiment over and over again.

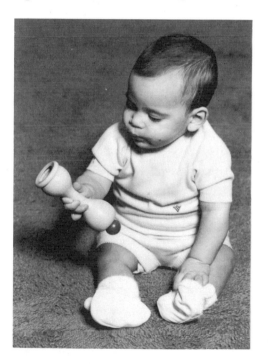

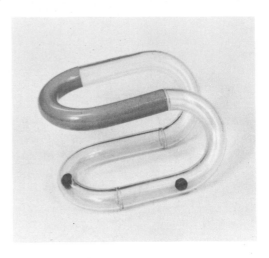

T U M B L E   T U B E _{TM}

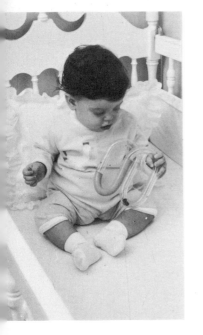

This learning toy also uses the action of gravity. Little colored balls roll through the transparent tubular pathway vanishing behind the colored section. They reappear again and again, carrying on a lively and fascinating life of their own which the baby can control. Rhythmic hand motion is put to practice. The balls go round and round, faster or slower as the baby learns to turn the toy. The baby must concentrate to achieve patterned movement. This is the baby's first truly three-dimensional toy that says something about the nature of objects in space. There is the pleasure of seeing and hearing and the satisfaction of solving a simple problem.

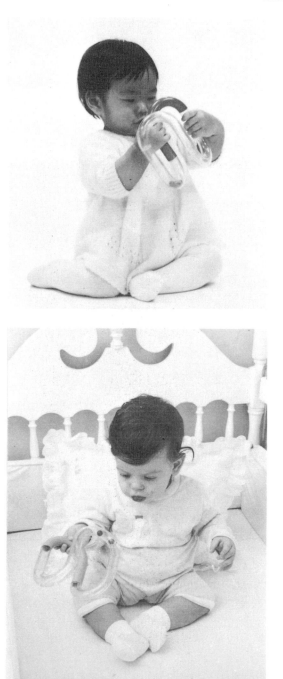

TODDLE ROLLER ™

The world expands as the baby begins to crawl about. Here is a toy that rolls ahead of him across the great spaces of the living room floor. The warm color lures him and the changing visual patterns and sound provide excitement and interest. As the toy rolls, colored shapes inside the plastic tube tumble and make noise. It can be picked up by its soft

rim and carried along. *Toddle Roller* is soft, roly-poly, light for its size, yet provides a feeling of shifting weight as the shapes move about. The toddler can hit it, pat it, fall on it, sit on it, look at it, listen to it and carry it about as a companion. This toy insists that the child moves. Through movement, the child gains control and coordination.

SEE-ME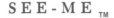

A play alone peek-a-boo toy. The funny-face clown with cut-outs for eyes and mouth and a bump for a nose swivels away revealing a mirror—and another face in the mirror—the baby's own. The swivel action can be repeated over and over offering another dimension of appearance and disappearance that could be called now-I-see-me, now-I-don't! While the shape of this easily cleanable toy, the handle, and even the nose satisfies a teething child, the main purpose of *See-Me* is to strengthen the child's sense of self.

The Part You Play: SERIES 3

Do not expect your child to react in any expected way with a new toy. If he is crawling when he first meets the *Toddle Roller* he may, indeed, start to push it immediately. But he is just as likely to look at it and leave it lie, or crawl away from it, or pick it up, put it down, and, for a while, forget all about it. Sooner or later he will discover all the interesting things about it.

This is true of the *Lollispoon* as well. It is a mistake to show impatience when the child does not seem to handle it in a way that will make the inner core slide back and forth. To introduce the Lollispoon you might hold your baby on your lap. Tip the Lollispoon back and forth. Relate to the child, laugh, talk—most important of all—enjoy the toy yourself. As soon as your baby wants to play with it, hand it over. Remember, the purpose of these toys, of any toy for this age, is one of discovery.

The *Tumble Tube* and *See-Me* allow the child to discover facts about the world, and the child does not approach things in the same way as an adult. Chances are the most likely reaction will be for the child to put them to his mouth. To us the miracle of gravity seems quite ordinary; a face in a mirror or something appearing and disappearing are explainable, everyday sorts of things that are not wondered about by the adult. But to the young child they are fascinating mysteries that he needs to solve for himself. Don't be impatient. Do encourage by giving your smiling approval whatever the initial approach to the toy may be. All these toys should give parents the opportunity to play with the child and share his wonder and delight.

Growth Objectives: MONTHS *9 to 12*

Most children, by now, are experienced creepers, are more and more mobile. Now they can pull themselves to a standing position and they soon learn the trick of low-ering themselves down, instead of tumbling back to a sitting position. Balance is more of a problem than the ability to stand and move forward.

Children in this age period begin to pay attention to some words, and the words may even have an effect on their behavior. Many children toward the end of this first year can say perhaps two words, some more, some none. But not long after this, if they are not using words themselves, they are aware of a great range of meaning expressed by language, gesture and facial expressions.

They are also great imitators and they will repeat ac-tions when the actions seem to meet with approval. The children, then, try to imitate words and gestures; hold crayons and try to scribble; learn to hold a cup and to drink from it. Soon they are cooperating in useful acts, helping to dress or to feed themelves. Also, through imitation, they will learn to clap hands, wave bye-bye, and so forth.

This is a period of exploration of objects and space using the eyes, ears, fingers and mouth. The child is studying the inside and outside of things, and their look, feel, sound and behavior. They drop, throw, push and pull things systematically to study what happens.

A child can now pick up an object the size of a quarter and can place it, with precision, in a small area. This skill continues to develop throughout this time period. By the end of it, the child can use and control the fingers independently, especially the index finger. Heavier things can be held.

Sometime during this period the child finds that there is a relation between two objects in space, for instance, one object resting upon the other. It is discovered that the top one can be reached by moving the bottom one. This may seem a small thing, indeed—but it is not. It is true experimentation. Your child is studying cause and effect—"I do this, and this happens." "I do that, and that happens." And this is the way of the world.

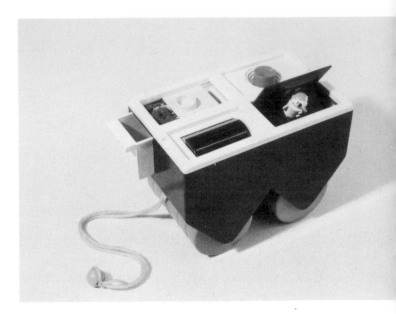

The Right Toy At
The Right Time SERIES 4

S M A R T   C A R T _{TM}

Here is a pull toy, a turning toy that makes delightful noises, a standing toy which when placed upright offers a variety of knobs, buttons, a sliding door, a secret drawer, a mirror, a hidden picture, sound rollers, a pull toy, and even a jack-in-the-box and a music wheel. All of these offer surprises that are totally delightful to the approaching one year old. He is eager to try out his new

abilities—better finger dexterity and increasing strength—on just such a wealth of fascinating devices. This is a whole bank of toys rolled into one. And it is beautiful to look at, too. Its lively contrasting colors and many interesting shapes offer the child a host of eye-hand coordination activities that help to develop observation and understanding of cause and effect.

MY POCKET BOOK ™

A very first picture book for baby. A book that can be changed as often as your child likes. Each of the eight clear plastic pages is a pocket which can hold a photograph of a member of the family, a leaf, a feather, a brightly colored label, a clipping from a magazine—anything that is fun to look at and interesting to talk about. A series of full color insert cards are included and are filled with detailed pictures of clothing, animals, food and objects which help stimulate a growing vocabulary. This book grows in interest and variety as your child grows. It helps to introduce the wonderful world of storybooks that will come later on.

The Part You Play: SERIES 4

Whether we admit it or not, we grown-ups can still be fascinated by children's toys. We want to play with them ourselves, and we know just how to pull things out and push things in and how to jiggle them so they make nice noises, and so on. Deep down inside of us, though goodness knows we would never admit it even to ourselves, we derive great satisfaction from the accomplishment. So play with your baby! Show your enjoyment! The *Smart Cart* is a great play-together toy. Hide something in the drawer. Turn the toy over and twirl the rollers. Push the squeaker button. Enjoy your baby's response!

Your baby doesn't know how to use a toy when it is first received and may not, for some time to come, do all the things with it you know can be done. But keep in mind that the purpose of the *Smart Cart* is to encourage the child to explore the physical world and learn about its behavior, to become more dexterous with the fingers, and most of all to gain pleasure and self-satisfaction at

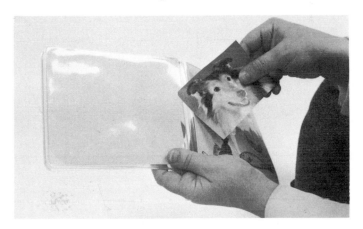

any level from the learning experience. Introduce the new toy with a smile and not with a course of instruction. Do not be concerned, or think your child is less developed than some other child you know, because his or her approach is different.

This is a good toy to take on trips. As the child gains confidence in walking there will be the enjoyment of pulling the toy along.

My Pocket Book requires your participation. All kinds of brightly colored patterns and pictures can be slipped into the clear plastic, pocket-pages: pictures, magazine cut-outs, labels from cans, postcards, alphabet letters, numbers and photographs of family members. (The child will not recognise people immediately, but after awhile, and often suddenly, he will become aware that they are pictures of people known and loved by him). In addition, the insert cards offer many pictures to point at and talk about with your baby. These should be changed periodically, to stimulate new interest. Variety in this instance is important, but the cards and pictures should not be changed daily. The child also needs the familiar and often, too many changes too quickly are distressing. Later, first drawings or scribble attempts are good things to add, giving the child a feeling that his efforts are liked and are worth keeping.

THE 2ND YEAR

NOW YOUR BABY IS ONE YEAR OLD, and he or she is already established as an individual. By the first birthday children show much variation in the rate of their development. Some can balance themselves well and are walking. Other children are barely beginning to walk—launching themselves forward—teetering a few steps before plunking down again. Others at this age may only pull themselves up from a sitting position, holding onto the rail or playpen or crib. The world they can see standing up is delightfully different than the world from floor level. They may spend many days just holding on without attempting to walk, studying this newly discovered aspect of reality. Still other children continue to crawl. Many one-year olds, even though they have mastered walking, choose to crawl whenever they want to move quickly.

MOBILITY IS THE THING! All of these children are either mobile, or soon will be. Because of this their world becomes wider. The objects they can observe at a distance or explore close up become more varied. The world has speeded up, has gained color and solidity for the child as soon as he becomes able to move with greater freedom. Sense perceptions must now react to the chance encounter of a variety of objects, not just those objects chosen and introduced by familiar adults.

THE TIME FOR CAUTION is here. Your baby is adventuresome—into everything. Mothers are well advised to clear low tables and shelves of things that can be broken, tasted, smeared, or thrown. A check of the living space should be made for anything that can harm a child: jagged or sharp instruments or tools, including kitchen and sewing implements; poisons and poisonous household chemicals. Make an inventory of your home. Do you use ant paste or roach powder? Is paint flaking off the wall where your baby can reach it? Have you been storing turpentine, alcohol, cleaning fluids, Clorox and the like in easy-to-get-to kitchen or bathroom cabinets? Anything small enough to be inhaled or swallowed should also be moved out of your child's reach. It is important, however, for you to make a distinction between healthy caution and nervous over-protectiveness.

REFINEMENT OF OTHER MOTOR SKILLS comes with greater mobility. Finger grasp becomes more specific and the hand stronger. Children strain to lift things which seem to them very big: a board, a book, a stone. They are fascinated with small things as well, and pursue an ant across the porch, sometimes trying to pick it up, sometimes stamping on it firmly and fiercely. Small things—a bead, a tiny ball, a flower, a shell—attract their interest and they work at trying to grasp them and hold them. Later on in the second year they can begin to deal with toys that come apart and can be put together. They are able to make marks on paper with a crayon.

Drawing at first is a muscular exercise rather than any form of representation, and the size of the swooping lines gives the child his sense of power.

THE CHILD PAST ONE begins to be aware of differences in size. He fills a container with objects, dumps it out, and starts again—completely absorbed. He is still intrigued and amazed when one thing really falls down into another. Will it happen again? He isn't sure. He tries it out all over again, and so after many trials he is convinced that X will always go into Y. At first the sizes must be markedly different, but later the differences become smaller and more precise, and in time he can even do a simple form-board puzzle. The circle, of course, is fitted first, because it has no corners to get in the way; then after a long time, the square, and finally the sharp and difficult triangle. Learning to understand and manipulate shapes and sizes is a major task that will occupy him for a long time to come, but this second year is when it begins.

OBJECT PERMANENCE DEVELOPS during the second year. This term is used by psychologists to explain the young child's dawning awareness that most things have solidity, are real and reliable, the sense that they will not vanish forever, even if they are not constantly present. For instance, Mother leaves the room, but now Johnny knows that she will come back again. He even looks, from time to time, at the door through which she is expected to reappear.

Children now begin to understand the relationship of one object to another though they are not directly in contact with either. Mother has left the plate of cookies on the table out of Peggy's reach. Peggy grabs the cloth and pulls it off the table. She knows that the plate of

cookies will come down with it and she uses this knowledge to get what she wants. It marks a great advance
in her understanding—though her mother may not
greet the mess with total approval. During this year children become more and more conscious of the laws which
govern the physical world. They will go on learning these
rules for many years, but now is when it begins. Each
time your child tests out a theory and learns that it is, or
isn't, so something is learned. A sense of the world as a
trustworthy place which can be relied upon to behave in
an expected way grows as your child's understanding
continues to advance.

PARENTS ARE MOST IMPORTANT during this
year. This is a period when the child learns to live as a
person among other people—he or she becomes aware
of having a place as a member of society. But this is not
an easy matter. The important adults in his life are asking the immature one-to-two-year-old to do a most difficult thing: to begin to give up impulsive, egocentric behavior and live according to the superimposed rules of
the family. Parents, especially the mother, must offer
encouragement and support, be responsive, and offer a
pattern of behavior to follow. Mother must be consistent.
This does not mean the rigid consistency of petty rules,
but a consistent attitude so that the child knows what to
expect and, at the same time, feels a sense of some freedom of choice.

A child responds to such a nurturing adult with trust
and deepening affection. Angry, fearful or even sadistic
emotions resulting from real frustrations—"I'm not big
enough." "I can't reach it!" "I can't understand!"— are
modified because the child is aware of being loved. It
is an awareness that is carried over even when mother
limits or restrains actions or gives a reprimand.

TOILET TRAINING is the major socializing task that is actively undertaken around sixteen months of age. At this time the child is asked to control a natural function which has always before taken place naturally, simply, with no need for thought. Why should he bother? The best reason, the most effective motivation is the desire to please mother. For her approval, the effort to gain control is made. This is the pattern for further socializing: the giving up of something easy, pleasant and undemanding for behavior that does not come as easily, but brings approval and more complete participation in the life of the group. Gradually, the child establishes the desired control, and a vague, physical sense of self becomes stronger and more defined.

WHAT DID BABY SAY? Almost overnight, it seems, your child is beginning to talk. Once walking is established and toilet training is begun, he makes rapid advances in language.

This burst of vocal progress has been led up to by preliminary steps evident throughout the second year. Typically, at about twelve months, the child is producing a stream of jargon. Here and there, the attentive adult distinguishes what seems to be a known word—*da-da, mama, daw* for dog, *bay* for baby. These "words" may or may not be accurately used, however. They generally have broader meanings than the actual words they approximate. For example, *daw* may mean every animal the child sees. This jargon is easily mistaken for actual language. Pauses, emphasis, tonal variations, all are perfect, as if a conversation were heard too far away to distinguished words. The child is playing with the sounds he hears around him, imitating language, preparing palate, larynx and facial muscles for true speech.

BABY IS TALKING, really talking now! Suddenly real words begin to be heard in what has been a field of sound. Two and three word sentences begin to be used. Jimmy really wants to communicate. Mary Ann understands much of what is said and responds to the spoken word. This final stage—actual speech—does not usually appear earlier than 18 months, more often around the second birthday and sometimes not until later—all in thoroughly normal children. When it happens, it marks a major advance. Now Jimmy and Mary Ann are able to deal with the world not only through action, but through symbols. Adults can help these newly verbal children by including them in conversation and exchanging ideas no matter how simple, at the same time suggesting words to them for thoughts and feelings they wish to express.

"I AM ME," says your child. Throughout this year your child's understanding of himself or herself as a person is taking shape from many, many tangible experiences: playing with fingers and toes, running, lying down, falling, rolling, being held and hugged, climbing, balancing. Awareness of self as a physical reality is building: "I am so big, so tall, my arms stretch so wide." "I can take steps as big as this. I can walk slowly or run fast." "I am Chris," or, "I am Pam." Pam is aware that she is loved—that she is precious to the adults in her family. Chris feels loved too, and knows that he is good —but that sometimes he is naughty. It is important for the child to recognize the parent's disapproval as real— an unhappy but not a fatal occurrence. The fact that sometimes Mother can disapprove can come as a startling surprise, but something is learned through it. There are times when disapproval is more or less expected. Chris or Pam will know that something is not supposed to be done, but will do it anyway. Reality is discovered through such experiences. And amongst other things, the child learns about anger and the fact that anger cannot really shrivel up the world!

THERE IS DELIGHT for children in learning words about themselves—my nose, my eyes, my mouth—my tongue is inside my mouth—see! these are my fingers, toes and elbows and knees. Human beings are language-using creatures and so such words add to their sense of self, in a very special way.

"LET ME DO IT MYSELF," your child will say. The growing feeling of being a person is often expressed in a drive towards autonomy, of not needing help from others. "Me feed myself!" is a statement Mother will be likely to hear as soon as her child is able to say the words. There will be scrambled egg on the bib, the child, the tray and the floor, and milk dripping down the chair leg—and mother may be distraught. There can be moderation in all things, but it is well to allow as much autonomous action as possible. It, too, is an expression of the vital, growing sense of being an individual. To attain it is worth suffering quite a number of messes.

AT THE CLOSE of the second year, a separate person and an actively participating member of the social group has begun to emerge. The child walks, is beginning to talk, imitates adults, explores the world within reach, sometimes with little judgment, but still with enormous interest and energy. In a thousand ways, your child is reaching out and learning.

Discovering the World through Toys

Growth Objectives: MONTHS 12 to 15

After the first birthday, generally following the development of walking, children usually begin to progress in language. Crying, babbling, cooing have gone on since the beginning of life. Perhaps a few pseudo words—da-da, ma-ma—have been spoken, but in spite of the excitement with which these are received, they are generally only sounds that happen to resemble words. They become meaningful only because of the enthusiastic reception they receive. It is as if the baby felt, "Wow! that got a big response—I'll do it again!" But now true words begin to appear, at first only a few—but show-

ing that now the child is really moving toward true attempts to communicate.

At the same time that children begin to work at developing language, they are becoming more sure of the permanence of things. Now they know that familiar things and people out-of-sight, out-of-hearing have not vanished all together. They are only invisible or silent for the moment, but still exist. This is a major piece of learning. A person's faith in the reliability of the physical world depends on having learned it through many experiences.

These months in your child's life are active, indeed. The baby is mobile, "into everything," exploring, opening and shutting, putting in and taking out, picking up and setting down. Many little things may interest him more than a single larger one. Pebbles, acorns, small blocks are fun to pick up and drop over and over again, and this is the beginning of understanding the concept of quantity. Learning to "let go" of an object is also a challenge.

The child is also becoming able to perform an action or make a gesture that he is not able to see himself do, as for example, scratching the ear or touching nose and chin. Gestures of this kind are things we take for granted. But they can only occur as a result of advances in the child's sense of his own body and his ability to imitate others. Like the recognition that objects are permanent, they indicate the development of mental images, basic to true thought.

The Right Toy At The Right Time: SERIES 5

E L E P H O N E ™

Here is an appealing, soft and cuddly friend to be loved as well as played with—a really original toy telephone. This is a language-readiness toy that allows your child to imitate the grown-up world of Mommy and Daddy, stimulating imitation of the sound of adult conversation patterns even before the child is able to form more than a word

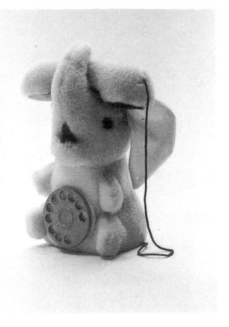

or two. The Elephone will have a long life, useful during the first months of the second year to increase the child's readiness to use words. And, for a long time to come, Elephone will be a dramatic means of stimulating language and growth through imaginative play. Its movable, numbered dial turns and makes a noise just like the real thing adding play value for nimble fingers.

BOWLS AND BALLS ™

This toy lends itself to being used at several levels of difficulty and so is able to challenge the child for several months beyond this three-month period. Now, it will meet the child's need to manipulate, to put in and take out, to explore size and shape by seeing what will go into what and how. Arranged with the funnel leading down into the container, the balls easily drop down inside; turn the funnel the other side up and the problem becomes more complex, to be used in a later stage of advancement. Still later, the child learns to insert the balls from the side. Either way the funnel is placed, *Bowls and Balls* is

designed to allow the baby the experiences of seeing a ball disappear into a container and then discovering that it did not really vanish, but is down inside. The recurrent discovery that the balls are really there is intensely pleasant to a child. Add to this the delight of controlling and manipulating, and the stimulus of constantly changing patterns created by the color and form of the balls against the container. Here is a toy intensely involving for the just-turned one-year-old. It will have lasting fascination for months to come as the child explores the various ways of stacking, nesting and filling the containers.

The Part You Play: SERIES 5

Elephone asks for participation on your part. Pretend to dial, to talk over the *Elephone* yourself when you introduce this toy. Continue using it in play situations with your child. Make an announcement, suggestion or the like. For example: "Ring, ring, ring. Hello Nancy, this is Mommy. Let's get dressed now and go shopping." If your child is phoning you, pretend to answer. Show your own pleasure in talking and listening to your child.

When you first give *Bowls and Balls* to your child show the way the balls drop through the funnel into the container when the funnel leads down. Drop them in and take them out several times when you have the child's interest. At this time, exclaim about the pretty colors and name them as you drop them in. "Look at the red ball. Where did it go? Oh, here it is!" Of course, don't expect your child to begin to identify colors immediately.

Do not be surprised when your child takes over. And, if the balls are used to roll along the floor or simply for dropping and picking up, these too, are physical facts, and ones which your child may be more interested in at the moment.

When the child is ready for it the funnel can be turned upside down and a whole new game of manipulation is there to test improved skills. You may discover that Johnny has done this all by himself and is handling this new game very well. However, he may discover that the funnel can be turned around but not be able to drop the balls into the smaller hole. If so, avoid frustrating him and tactfully show him that he can return the funnel to its former position. Let your child play in the way that offers personal satisfaction.

Growth Objectives:
MONTHS 15 to 18

As you have discovered, not just through reading these pages, but through the very practical experience of being a parent, your child is an individual developing rapidly in one area at one time, more slowly in another, and continually shifting emphasis. As each month goes by, the more individual and unique that development becomes.

This book can only generalize, so it is important to realize that what is said will often agree, but sometimes disagree with observable changes in your own child's progress. Don't pat yourself on the back and say, "Goodness, Lisa is talking a blue streak, and most children are just beginning to form two or three word sentences at her age." But most of all, don't become distressed if a generalization indicates that your child's progress in an area is slower than the norm: for instance, the book says, "The child is running all over the place and into everything," but your child is still crawling. He may be developing in some related but not identical area of growth. For example, he may be sitting and developing a marvelous dexterity with his fingers. "He can hold a pencil and draw fine lines, but oh dear! he cannot take more than one step or two without being helped." If you do have a genuine concern, your pediatrician is the person to consult.

The typical fifteen- to eighteen-month-old child is usually intensely active. This toddler is very often running, climbing up and down stairs, going into and out of nooks, constantly varying movements, testing all the possibilities of any situation. The feet are still wide apart when walking, maintaining a broad base on which to balance the body, which is not yet wholly erect when the child is standing still. Large muscle activity is often more fascinating than small muscle use (working with fingers, for example).

The one-and-a-half year old is difficult to direct or control, because at this age the child has not yet learned how to inhibit actions. But, on the other hand, his attention can be diverted quite easily. The child's interest fastens quickly on anything that presents itself and shifts just as quickly when some other fascination is offered.

There is a beginning of understanding and antic-

ipation of how things might work. The child is becoming able to generalize because of earlier experiences. There is also progress in arranging and in his understanding that some things can be grouped together because of sameness—categorization. There is a growing awareness of color, too. Now more and more new words are being learned and old words take on deeper shades of meaning. Books and conversation are satisfying and important at this time.

The Right Toy At The Right Time: SERIES 6

S U P E R H O U N D _{TM}

This is the right age for a pull-toy, and here is one of enormous charm. *Super-hound's* back is a sorting box with three differently shaped holes into which the small blocks included as part of this toy can be inserted. The child can reach in and find the blocks again—repeating the action over and over.

The youngest children will be able to make the circular form fit successfully before they can manage the square or triangle; somewhat older children, with satisfying effort, will manage the square and still older children will gain a real feeling of triumph when they manage to

fit the triangle into place. There is enough challenge here to occupy several months of growth in fine muscle control and eye and hand coordination. *Superhound's* tail holds a stack of brightly colored, graduated rings. At first, children will concentrate on taking the rings off the tail and getting them back on in any order. Later on, placing them on the tail in sequence will be something to try for.

This is an early categorization toy which provides learning in the areas of size, form and color. The blocks or rings may be played with alone, but in connection with *Superhound* their meaning has new dimensions. From his squeaker nose to his gaily colored tail he is a pet toddlers will enjoy having along on their increasingly adventurous expeditions.

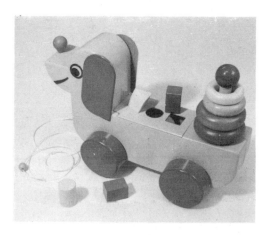

SUPERHOUND'S BUSY DAY

A delightful companion to *Superhound,* this wipe-clean panorama book tells a simple story about Superhound's travels. It is a story about the senses. Superhound sees, smells, tastes, touches and hears many things as he goes through the woods, a farm and the streets of town. The reverse side of the book shows a panorama view of where he has been. In time, the older child will be able to relate the sequence of activities by pointing out details in the scene. This is a sturdy book constructed in a practical and unusual format.

The Part You Play: SERIES 6

These toys are planned to motivate and stimulate intellectual growth and motor coordination. The "Wonder of Growing" Book explains growth patterns and when and in what way each toy relates to these. You will want to use them to enhance your child's growth. Observe and listen—listen to what your child is telling you with actions as well as words. Help him explore and use the toys with your own loving understanding as the best guide.

With *Superhound,* show him how to pull it. Take the shapes out and put them in again, letting the child take over if he wants to handle them on his own. Show him that the rings can be lifted off the tail. If Jimmy or Sally just wants to play with the rings or the blocks, enjoy that aspect of the toy with him or her. If the rings are desired back on the tail, again be helpful, but do no more than seems to be demanded. Don't be critical of attempts that fail. Sooner or later your child will discover relationships.

In *Superhound's Busy Day* do not expect your child to comprehend all the facets immediately. These will unfold in weeks and months to come. The appeal at the beginning will probably be the individual panels which describe a particular sense experience. The story line is purposely brief allowing the parent to create conversation with the child—unique conversation fitting the individual needs and experiences of your child. "Doesn't the dog look like our Brownie?" "What is he smelling with his nose? Where is your nose?"

In the beginning, labeling is appropriate and the book offers ample opportunity for this. Later, when the child

seems interested, an effort can be made to talk about sequence. "What happens next?"

As more books are presented to your child, you will develop your own techniques of questioning—"picture reading," and telling of stories in response to your child. Doing what is comfortable is important. With your involvement you engage the child's attention. Above all, should attention wander, do not insist that the book be finished.

Superhound's Busy Day is also a good book for your child to look at by himself. It is sturdy and should be out with the rest of the toys. You can spread it out and stand it up on the floor, bureau or play-pen for easy viewing.

Growth Objectives: MONTHS *18 to 21*

It is not so easy, now, to see progress, but it is going on all the time. The leaps are often mental ones. Connections are being made based on experience and the growing ability to think with symbols. Grandmother who hasn't seen the baby in several months, she will exclaim, "Look at the way Bobby is walking like a little man, now!" Mother hasn't noticed that he is standing up straight or keeping his feet closer together. It all happened so gradually. Or another grandmother will remark, "Lisa is talking now—whole sentences! And she knows just what I'm saying!"

The child, at this age, is intensely active, energetic, exploring, pushing, pulling, carrying, putting in and taking out. More and more he imitates the activity going on in the home—anxious to take part in what he sees going on around him. Now he begins to be capable of figuring out problems entirely in his head. No longer does he have to depend completely on physical manipulation to solve his questions—how to reach the ball, open the door, put on mittens.

Words are still labels—the word dog, *for instance, may stand for all animals—but idea words—*bad, good, funny, happy, more, want *are beginning to be understood and will soon be used.*

Physical puzzles are solvable—opening a box; pulling out a drawer; moving one thing to get at another. There is a knowledge of what things are used for. The ability to group things is growing.

The Right Toy
At The Right Time: SERIES 7

LOOK AND LEARN
SHAPE BOOKS AND
POSTERS

The child's first set of "real" books offers words to listen to, and pictures to see that are full of absorbing information: pictures of baby animals, animal homes, cats and dogs, children and friendly lions, numbers and nursery rhymes. These sturdy, beautifully designed little books are just the right weight and shape to be carried about. They will be listened to and learned by heart. Learning to read is *not* their purpose, but they will enhance your child's readiness to tackle

reading later on with enthusiasm, because reading is presented here as a delightful experience.

Children who early in life find books friendly have a head start towards language competence in school. They already know that books can tell about things they want to know and that they make the world a more interesting place. The words in these little books build vocabulary, help to organize ideas and stimulate children to express themselves more accurately.

Four large posters printed in full color —on two non-tearable, wipe-off, plastic sheets—are included with the Look and Learn Shape Book Library.

There are four key subjects—conversation starters at a child's level: zoo animals with labels showing their names; a panoramic view of the city with trucks, cars, planes, trains and boats— things that move; and people, busy people at work and play. A third poster shows activities in a child's day, from morning until night. Delightful vignettes that small children can identify as things they do themselves show a variety of experiences a child enjoys at home. And last but not least, a labeled scene that illustrates and highlights parts of the body—an involving interest, an important learning for the child on the way to self-identity.

BLOX BOX ™

A new and orginal set of blocks for your child: light-weight, with rounded edges, yet sturdy. Their colors are deep and beautiful, each color a different size. Sizes are related: three of *these* are as long as two of *those*, four like *this one* as wide as *one of that*. The child is actually playing with quantities that relate to each other, with measurement and number, in an unstated but enormously valuable way. Can he make the house stand up? Then the walls must be of equal height, and the child discovers that so many of one size add up to so many of another size. Thus, the notion of equal amounts is born. But equally important to learning are the

hours of pleasure in building and knocking down, in creating towers, houses, roads, or just in making constructions for their own sake, for the challenge of building and balancing and the pleasure of using form and color to create pattern.

Another facet of this toy is object-permanence—an appearance and disappearance the child controls. The largest block is hollow and open at both ends. Drop the other blocks into it—they disappear. Pick up the big block and the smaller blocks tumble out on the floor. Or, the smaller blocks can be pushed through the tunnel and will appear at the other end. These actions will be repeated over and over again with variations. They are, in a very real sense, experiments.

The Part You Play: SERIES 7

Perhaps one of the best times to introduce a *Look and Learn Shape* Book to your child is before a nap or bedtime. Besides the other values inherent in these books, they also introduce the idea to your super-active offspring, that fun can be had while being quiet with someone loved. These books, however, should be available to your child during the day. Your child should be able to go to a shelf or window sill and select a book, pick a comfortable place to sit and "read."

Read the words to the child, perhaps pointing out a few as you do so. Help him to see that you are looking at those marks on the page and that they have meaning. Take a good deal of time with the pictures, talking about them together and showing your own pleasure. The pictures are rich in content. You will see many opportunities for comments—for ways of enriching your child's understanding of concepts such as big and little, over and under, up and down, and names of things. Expect that you will be asked, even, perhaps, wheedled into reading these books over and over—and after a while don't be surprised if you are expected to listen while your child pretends to read to you the words that have been learned by heart.

Hang the posters at your child's eye level, either one or both of them. They are colorful and attractive, and most of all they are conversation starters. Talk about them: "What is happening? Did we ever see that kind of animal? That's a big truck! Find the little girl's elbow. That car looks just like the one on the corner. See, it's time to take a nap. Look, that's the way baby helps mother." If your child is particularly interested in identifying parts of the body there are endless discussion possibilities using the labeled pictures that say *elbow, knee, toe* and so forth.

Turn the posters to the other side when you feel interest has reached a peak and is waning. Children at this age may lose interest for a while, and have it reawaken a few weeks later. Little by little they will begin to notice various details and will enjoy studying the illustrations and talking about them.

Blox Box is an "I-can-do-it-myself" toy for your child. Avoid taking over because you can see that that house is never going to stand up straight if you let the child alone. However, there are times, depending upon your child's personality, when a helpful hint by-passes frustration. If your child gets frustrated, and only if you know that helping out will be welcome, then do so. But there are many children who will become more irritated by this than they would be by succeeding or failing for themselves. Knowing your own child is of prime importance. Sometimes if he begins to be upset with trying to do something that is really too hard for him, the best thing to do is awaken his interest in something else, then when interest has shifted to the pull toy or some other favorite, put the *Blox Box* away for another day.

Growth Objectives: MONTHS 21 to 24

The child approaching two is leaving infancy behind and becoming a child in the full sense of the word. He is more mobile, better organized and more truly a language user than three months before. Now he can bend over without toppling on his face, although the tendency to lean forward while running is still there. Going up and down stairs is accomplished, but without alternating feet. Balls are kicked, but knee action hasn't completely developed, and typically, legs seem to turn into spaghetti when Mother tries to put on the snowboots.

Although as yet more involved in developing the large muscles, the child is improving in small muscle coodination needed to perform fine tasks. For instance, the child is now able to rotate his arm from the elbow, a needed skill for turning a door knob, unscrewing a lid and other operations of this kind. Better control allows the child to put one thing into another. And great delight is found in taking things apart and putting them together again.

The typical two-year-old is making great strides with language. The next year will see a basic grasp of the system of language, but already many words are truly meaningful. Verbal skills are supplemented by physical reality. There is still a great need to touch, fill, pour, squeeze, push, pull, and so forth, to learn the nature of the world about him.

This age marks the time when the child moves into the level of symbolic intelligence (not only under- standing about things but also, the idea *of things). It also marks the time when language more and more becomes the prime means of solving problems. Whereas before, the child was able to discover things and to imitate, now invention is possible. He can imagine how things ought to act.*

For instance, now the child can find something that is hidden under something else. Alice places one of her blocks on the chair. She goes to look for it because she has a visual picture in her mind of hav- ing placed it there. In the meantime, someone has covered it with a coat. No block can be seen. But at this age, Alice doesn't consider that it may have vanished forever. She darts a hand under the coat and finds the block right where she left it.

Tony has lost a ball. It has rolled away under the low cabinet, too far back to see or reach. But Tony can find ways of reaching it. He can fish it out with a stick. He has invented a ball-fisher-outer, an exten- sion of his own arm, just like that!

The Right Toy At The Right Time: SERIES 8

BUSY TRAIN ™

A more complex toy which offers an extraordinary variety of possible arrangements of form, size, and color. It can be taken apart and put together in a number of ways. It can be stacked or nested. Smaller elements can disappear down holes to be found and returned there again. It is a form puzzle, a construction toy, a pull or push toy, a problem solving toy, a dramatic play toy train big enough for a toy engineer to ride about in.

Category Train is a tremendous improvement over the traditional toy trains that can only be used for pushing accompanied by chugging noises though it serves in this capacity, as well. This train has a long life because it lends itself to being used in many different ways—from the simple to the complex as the child's skills increase.

COLOR LOOK BOOKS _{TM}

These three books: *My Red Look Book, My Yellow Look Book, My Blue Look Book* offer story ideas accompanied and emphasized by the impact of color. Red, yellow, blue, the primary colors, are explored in terms of the child's own experiences with weather, times of day, animals, toys, things that move and even moods. Each book builds towards greater awareness in the child's use of his eyes as he looks through the colored transparent window on each sturdy page. He sees his familiar world done over in greater awareness in the child's use of red, in blue and in yellow. Here is a language and a science experience, each strengthening the other.

The Part You Play: SERIES 8

Common sense and an understanding of your child can help make *Busy Train,* as well as other toys, an important pleasurable learning experience. There are many parts to this toy. They will tend to get spread around, and it is important that they do so. The train will be disassembled to be reassembled. Some of the pieces will be left lying where they have been taken out, and the whole game continued in some other place, the missing part forgotten. The child, at this age, needs space and should not be limited to a small play corner, but it is also true that grownups like to live in a relatively unlittered place, where they can walk down stairs or through a hall without turning an ankle on a small block or disc. Make the use of the toy pleasant and without too many restrictions, but also, make a game of finding the pieces and putting it all back together when playtime is finished. Show your child that it is fun to put things away, by asking for help, avoiding being critical of the help given, and expressing your own pleasure in doing something together.

When introducing the toy, it is important to show some of the possibilities. The funnel fits on all the tops. One cannister comes apart in three pieces. The elements stack. The tops can fit over the cylinder, and so on. Your child will experiment on his own, but now and again, you may want to open up another avenue for him to explore.

The brief stories in each of the *Look Books* have a built-in rhythm that will make remembering the words easy. Read the words and study the pictures. Ask your child to point out the yellow butterflies, or say, "Where is the red truck?" or, "Are all the umbrellas blue?" Picture reading is a reading-readiness skill. Show the child how to look through the colored transparent windows. Look through the window yourself and say what you see. "I see a red chair," or "I see a red cup that used to be blue," or, "I see you. Oh my goodness you are blue!" Then ask your child what he or she sees. The transparent windows on each page of each book allow children to see a different aspect of the reality they have come to be so familiar with and largely take for granted. The art of seeing, instead of merely looking, is an important art indeed.

THE 3RD YEAR

A SIGNIFICANT YEAR. As he nears his third birthday, your child is clearly *child,* no longer *baby.* Many of the qualities that make him a person in his own right come about as the result of essential developmental stages during these twelve months.

A TIME OF EXPANSION: he runs, jumps, climbs—his world continues to expand and become more diverse. He fingers, looks carefully at tiny things—a ladybug, a shiny pebble, a raindrop on the window. He listens intently and his world becomes more exact. He thinks more, reflects more than ever before, using his developing memory and his sharpening tool of language.

A TIME OF REFINEMENT: he can use his hands and fingers more accurately. Greater control comes as he handles—puts-in and takes-out, lifts and sets down, adjusts what he does with his body to the size, shape and weight of objects he uses. Now he begins to learn the differences between things which earlier he would have lumped together. His newly acquired stock of words helps here, and every experience adds to his understanding. To learn that a *kitty* is not a *doggie* is to begin to comprehend the world of four legged animals in a permanently important way.

A TIME OF ANGER: progress in becoming a whole person isn't always easy. There is normally a period between two and two-and-a-half when the most easy-going children become negative and difficult. "No" becomes the answer to almost everything: "No, I wont eat my breakfast . . . No, I won't go to bed . . . No! No! No!" It is as if the child can define and protect his emerging self only by turning down the most reasonable suggestions of others. Even pleasing suggestions may be rejected because the power of saying "No" is a greater benefit. For awhile, there is a swinging back and forth between the compliant, dependent baby behavior that is being left behind, and the strong powerful actions of the person the child sees himself to be in fantasy—wants to be, and yet is afraid of being.

A TIME OF FRUSTRATION: the world is full of antagonizing circumstances. The child has little ability to control or to quiet strong feelings. For instance, Alan has just learned to make his new tricycle go and is soaring along like a bird when, with a jarring thump, the back wheels get caught on a chair leg and there he is, hung up, unable to move, and the first few times it happens, totally in the dark about what to do. Of course, he is filled with fury! It is a great dark anger that seems huge and hot enough to swallow the world. Only gradually does he learn that the world continues as sunny and calm as before—unaware of its danger.

The feelings of the child at this time must be much like those of an adult who finds himself carried away on a powerful motorcycle with no notion of how he can turn the thing off. But with the two-and-a-half-year-old, the motorcycle is the self, the desires, the intense feelings that cannot be turned off. A blanket *no* to all things, good, bad and indifferent, sometimes seems to be the child's only method of asserting himself and his right to make choices.

A TIME OF STRESSES AND SUCCESSES: every child learns how to begin activities before learning how to terminate them; how to grasp things before being able to let go. But soon enough, activities begun are also brought to a successful close, and the *no* begins to be put aside for *yes*. The child gains a more relaxed ability to choose—to say *yes* to some things and *no* to others, as may be appropriate.

Though this year has its storms, aggressions, tantrums and sudden returns to pseudo-babyhood when pressures mount too high, much of it is also a very happy time. For most children, newfound balance and control of the body in moving is a source of enormous pleasure. Children run, roll, climb upstairs, cascade down on their stomachs, or bump down on their backsides, jump, flop onto soft things, bang one thing against another. Outside reality is being tested!

SPACE IS A NECESSITY: development may be affected if a child is limited to a small apartment without sufficient outdoor activity. Trips to park or playground, to the beach or the country are necessities for children at this age. The joy of rapid movement brings with it a sense of competence, of being able to cope. Through motion, active children define themselves, body image becomes more definite.

For families who live in constricted space, with neighbors close around them, it is difficult indeed not to "shush" a noisy, jumping two-and-a-half-year-old. The child's bounciness seems pointless, and the people downstairs are banging on the ceiling. Some "don'ts" are inevitable, but parents must realise that the need for motion is as real for the child of this age as the need for food and warmth. Inhibit Jimmy too much, and he becomes wild and destructive, with an edge of hysteria in his play. Be over-cautious with Julie and she may turn to fantasy too early before she has built a base in reality, before she has had the real experience of her body moving in space.

ACTIVITY ISN'T AIMLESS, though it may seem so. It is, in fact, providing a wealth of opportunity for the child to learn the nature of the physical world. These learnings have been going on all along, but now the physical being is more developed; the nervous system can take in and retain more information. The child is more in touch with the world outside: Paul hefts a chair with straining muscles and discovers "heavy"; blows a fluff of milkweed seeds and experiences "light"; stamps up bare wooden steps and contrasts this with the sounds of walking on covered floors; splashes in puddles; squishes in mud; wallows in snow; rolls in soft grass. So he learns about texture, weight, shape, volume and all the rest. He may not know the words with which to express the results of his explorations, but he is gaining awareness of the reality they stand for. Soon meaning and words will fuse.

WORDS are among the elements that shape this year of life. Linguists tell us that this third year is the crucial one for language development. This is when, given half a chance, the child somehow, no one knows quite how, absorbs the rules of language from conversations going on around him. Suddenly, Mother hears a sentence, a two word sentence: "Truck go"; a three word sentence: "Susan want supper"; then, any-number-of-word sentences. Typically, it happens fast. One day, the child is really non-verbal, though a few words are used and adults know they can speak and be understood. The next day or week the child has launched out, is a language-user! One of the great benchmarks of life has been attained. Without instruction, without fanfare, the human child has learned to do something no other living being can do. Only mankind talks. Use of language signifies a new manner of thinking. Now he begins to think as adults do, in images and symbols. Of course he has a long way to go before understanding and using adult laws of logic. His thought processes are still inconsistent, magical, everything considered in terms of self: "The moon follows me when I go for a walk." or, "Bad chair, make me fall." But these phrases show real thinking, none the less. The wise parent does not try to impose grown-up ways, but rather, listens, remembers and tries to see how the world looks to the child. This period of child thought verbalised is brief enough. It is a wonder and a joy to catch some of its flavor on the wing. Enjoy your child's new approach to reality.

I, ME, MY, JOHNNY, MARY are words that emphasize the sense of selfhood. Words and movement make children aware of themselves as individuals, help them to the understanding: "I am not the same as anyone else. I am not the property of anyone else." It is because of this growing sense of uniqueness that the child, although dearly loving his mother, father and other familiar people, also shows hate and rebellion.

A TIME FOR SEPARATENESS is here; it is not a casual thing. Up to this time the child's very being has been rooted in Mother. To leave her would have been impossible, a disaster. But now the child begins to experiment with leaving even the most beloved, and to try what it is like to go off on his or her own, across the room, into the next room, out into the yard to play. "I go now. Goodbye," and Richie takes off riding his trike down the immense spaces of the sidewalk. *He* must do the leaving. Mother must do the waiting. And it is all important that she wait there, just where she was left— cooking in the kitchen, sitting in the living room or on the porch or apartment house steps—to be rediscovered, to be returned to, all of two minutes later. Richie, and Rachel too, learn that they can go away and can come back home again, and home will still be there where they left it. On this certainty rests their future capacity to go out to face the world sure that the roots of self will not be lost in the process.

THE WORLD OF THINGS can be depended upon too. It is important to know that objects are faithful in their own way, that they too can be expected to behave predictably. The bed will stay where it is left, and will be soft, warm, cozy when it is returned to. Houses stay solid. Cars stay fast-moving—the qualities of things are reliable. Some things are the child's very own, and these things have great significance, for they help define the self. These are Jane's shoes, they do not fit anyone else in the family. This is Jane's spoon, cup, plate and no one else uses them. Some things are shared with others, but while Jane has them, they are hers: this is Jane's turn to use the record player, later, Susie can have it. Tommy also has to be sure that there are some things that are really his, permanently his; his teddy bear, his red truck, his fireman's hat, his blue balloon. He needs to know that other people cannot and will not take his things away. When this is learned, Tommy can begin to share. Very few two-year-olds can share, and most ought not to be expected to do so. They aren't ready and it only does harm to push. But when you see your Tommy or your Susie reaching out to give a shovel to another child in the sand pile, taking turns on the swing, or waiting, without protest, in line to use the slide, then you know that he or she is well along in gaining a sense of possession strong enough to allow the self-defining objects to be removed for awhile without losing the sense of self.

DADDY IS A BOY! MOMMY IS A GIRL! Another vital dimension of the personality is largely defined during this year: the dimension of sex. What it is to be a boy, what it is to be a girl; what it is to be daddies and mommies. Who men and women are and how they act begins to come clear. Parents are the models and they shape their children's lives in essential ways. If they themselves accept and are happy in their sex roles, their children will be the same. The three-year-old is not only *child*, but also, *boy* or *girl*.

PLAYING IS LEARNING. Because of enhanced motor and mental development, play takes on new richness. It is physically and intellectually more active. Games of running, tumbling and tussling are greatly enjoyed, although with much more freedom when involving a trusted adult than with peers. Other children are of great interest, but as subjects to be observed rather than played with. The almost-three-year-old plays as an individual even though physically part of a group. But individual play is now enhanced by greater capabilities.

Imaginative play can truly begin, for the child possesses words and images, memories and emotions to put into it. These are added to the sheer physical handling of objects: now the hammer is more than just a tool for pounding, it is for pounding a nail, building a boat; and fists are not made just for the feel of punching, but for killing a make-believe bear, or punishing a real bad boy. Aggressions are part of the scene, and when they come out, though rough and crude in fantasy form, they can be helpful for they often allow a child who has been actively negative to behave better in real life. Some of that fierceness can be siphoned off in dramatic play. Children are going through a major identification process with their parents, particularly the parent of the same sex. Much of this major life task is expressed in the vivid meaningful play that they carry on with blocks, or dolls, or vehicles, or anything that lies at hand.

THIS IS A WONDERFUL YEAR! Keep your sense of humor and sense of wonder and enjoy observing your child become far more of a person, in touch with other people and the world. Remember when your child seems more difficult to handle, that he is now more vulnerable because feelings are deeper than the year before. A fascinating, complex, active human being already trying out all the major themes that will run throughout life, is the child about to turn three.

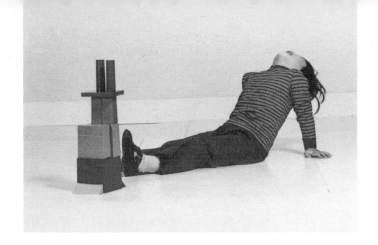

Discovering the World through Toys

Growth Objectives: **MONTHS 24 to 27**

The child going into his third year of life is an individual. Yet even more this year than in the first two years of life, children develop in different ways, at different tempos. To say that a child at twenty-six months is doing or behaving in this way or another way is like saying that every twenty-six month old wears the same size shoes. It is apparent that children vary in physical size. It is also true that they vary in behavior, in learned skills, in perceptions and in every other dimension.

The skills and concepts discussed here apply to the two-to-three-year-old, but when we suggest that they occur during a specific time period, for instance between 24 and 27 months, these are merely rough rules-of-thumb. Vary them to fit your child. If your child seems to be far more or far less active than is suggested as typical for the time period, you should not feel unduly delighted or overly concerned. He is proceeding according to his inner timetable and this is as it should be.

Our typical child just past his second birthday is active and increasingly well-coordinated—he can walk up and down stairs alone, for example, still stepping with both feet onto one step before tackling the next. Balance has improved. Everything is an invitation to activity. Boxes are to be climbed upon. Low walls are to be walked along holding on to a big person's hand. Heavy things are to be pulled or pushed.

Close to the second birthday (sometimes before, sometimes after) most children go into an intense language-learning and experimenting period. The number of words known increases rapidly and the child experiments with creating sentences. While only two words long and incomplete, they stand for much longer thoughts and show a great mental advance. This is, of course, a general statement. Some children of this age are not yet speaking and others are even more verbal than described. The year ahead, however, is an important time in language development when the child absorbs the basic rules of syntax from the adult society, without, of course, realizing this in a conscious way.

Now Jeff and Mary refer to themselves by name, and can often tell mother when there is a need to

go to the bathroom. Daytime accidents are fewer, but most children of this age still need diapers at bedtime.

The two-year-old is becoming more social and more affectionate although in an unsupervised situation, or when over-tired, he can become quite violent. Jeff is dependent on his mother and tries to demand all her attention, especially when other people are present. Mary is timid with strangers, but this is actually a sign of her increased awareness of people. Two-year-olds enjoy people, are friendly as soon as they feel at ease and are delighted when there is a chance to play with another child. After about twenty minutes, though, conflict can erupt and must be handled by the adult promptly, for there is no limit to spontaneous aggression. Children at *this age are unaware that hair-pulling or hitting with a shovel can hurt. The adult must step in and separate the tusslers while it is still a friendly, puppy sort of conflict. No punishment—just a friendly hug to each and something to divert their attention. "Don't hit Teddy—it hurts" must be repeated many times before the lesson is absorbed.*

Along with language development comes great improvement in small muscle coordination. Pages of a book can be turned now, one by one, without tearing. And now the spoon goes into the mouth without dropping most of the food on the way.

Little things that move and turn are found to be intriguing and so are larger things which fit together and twist apart. The wrists have developed to the point where soon, if not as yet, door knobs will be turnable, and this skill will be practiced endlessly. We have been told that small children have short spans of attention and so they do, generally. But at the moment when a new skill becomes possible, they will practice it with phenomenal concentration.

These advances in coordination skills and thinking give the child an opportunity to engage in much more complicated and varied activities. Experimentation can take place—how do things work? Concentration is on the increase and now the child is ready to observe an action or reaction with deeper interest. Materials stimulate curiosity and new capabilities allow the child to explore to his satisfaction.

The Right Toy
At The Right Time: SERIES 9

WATER WORKS _{TM}

This toy challenges the child in many areas of small muscle coordination and concept development and continues to be a challenge as the child grows. Here is a small child's laboratory—a dozen or more toys in one that makes bathtime one of the most exciting and creative experiences of the day. The bath becomes a time for fun, a period of effortless learning, of exciting exploration. What is water? What does it do? Why does it flow? Why does it move things? Why does it feel like rain as it falls through the sieve. What is a bubble? Why, why, why?

Playing with water, in the soak-proof area of the bath tub, will develop your child's awareness of weight, of volume, of force, of the interaction of water and air as water is poured through air or air is carried down into water to bubble back up to the surface again. The individual parts of this toy can be taken apart and played with separately, can be assembled, disassembled and reassembled in a multitude of ways. The housing, attached by three suction cups to the bathroom wall or bathtub side can remain permanently in position or

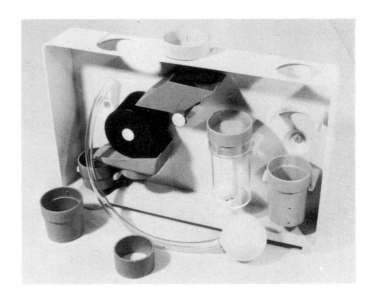

is easily removable. It can either be an integral part of the play laboratory experience, or, when receptacles are used separately in the bath, becomes a housekeeping unit, training the smaller child to put away his toys when finished.

This one durable toy with its many learning dimensions will offer excitement, interest and variety for months, perhaps years to come. The child at any level of development will be able to use the toy effectively without frustration. As he grows new ways of using the components will become apparent.

The Part You Play: SERIES 9

Introduce this toy as a surprise by placing it in position in the tub just before bathtime. In this way the toy's possibilities in water are immediately seen.

The chances are that the first reaction will be to take out the various receptacles and float them in the bath. Let this happen for several bath periods. There will be things for the child to learn about each part in this way. However, when bathtime is over, on the first day and for as long as it is necessary, while the child is still in the tub, suggest putting things back in place—and help, making it a game. This activity not only trains the child to "put things away" but is also a good experience in visualizing where things fit.

You might open up the possibilities of the bulb syringe by squeezing it, allowing it to fill with water and then using it to help wet down a hand or a knee before applying soap. The plastic tube can be submerged completely, allowing it to fill with water, stopping the water from running out by placing a finger over each end. Or a bubble can be captured and watched.

The child can pour water through a funnel or sieve and see the difference. The receptable with the three holes sends three sprays arching in the air, then two and finally one and then the water is gone. Water can be observed in the transparent jar and the floating ball rises closer to the top with each addition of water. The child can scoop water into a cup, pour from one cup to another, funnel water from one to another as well, and so on.

Whenever your child seems ready—it may be the day the toy is received, or a week or more later, show what happens when water is poured through the hole in the housing. Show how the force of the water tips the tipping trough that then pours water on the waterwheel making it rotate; thereby dumping water into the scoop and then down back into the tub.

On the other side of the tipping trough, the child can place a sieve, funnel or any of the other receptacles including the clear plastic cannister with the ball. Or, water can be poured through a hole at the top of the case sending it into and through a series of vessels, sieves, funnels, scoops, cups etc. These water systems can be changed each time using different combinations of vessels and new reactions can be observed.

All of these receptacles are modular, that is, they can fit together and be capped in various ways using the removable collar which fits all of them. This aspect of the design adds even more play variety since the child can construct many interesting vessels—a cup with a funnel top, a cup with a sieve top and so on.

The parent's role is to open up new possibilities for the child. Remember that these are numerous and parents should be sensitive to what the child seems to be enjoying at the time and not try to demonstrate complicated procedures when the child is not ready for them.

A two-year-old should not be left alone in the bath. If, however, the child is steady enough sitting down to play without your hovering directly over the tub, place *Water Works* on the side within easy reach of the *seated* child. *Water Works* is equally adaptable to sand. It can be used in a sand box or on the beach.

Growth Objectives: MONTHS 27 to 30

Mothers are becoming more and more aware now that they are sharing the home with someone whose responses are quite unpredictable. The child is three months bigger, stronger, more energetic physically, and three months more self-assertive. All that two-year-old energy may have tired you before, but the energy level is still on the way up!

As the child approaches the two-and-a-half year mark there is more of everything—liveliness, mobility, aggression, curiosity, and possessiveness. While there is a strong sense of personal possession—"That's mine!" whether it is or not—there is no reliability when it comes to other people's property. The time has come when breakables, antiques, prized bric-a-brac must be placed out of reach. At the same time, the living room should not be so stripped down that the child never learns how to be careful of the ashtray on the coffee table, the candle in the candle-stick holder. The child who turns mother's work basket upside down scattering its contents, is at the same time building taller, more stable structures with blocks.

It is normal at this age for a child to feel a great aversion to sharing equipment or toys. In large families or in nursery groups there should be enough of any particularly alluring object to go around. At this age, a child truly cannot share. His intense and un-

reasonable sense of ownership is a way station on the road to generosity. Before possessions can be used in common, a feeling of security about them must exist. The need to own is also a sign of growing ego-strength, of awareness of self. It is as if the child were saying, "I am me because this is mine!" Be tolerant of this phase, it will not last very long.

Books are an ideal means of relating closely to your child. Sharing a storybook provides a sense of security and stimulates language growth by feeding the child's growing appetite for new words and thoughts. Children enjoy looking at books by themselves too. "Look, I am big. I am 'reading' my own book!

Children, at this age, love to play outdoors and are delighted with the company of other children. But though they are friendly, an adult should be near-by and attentive, for play may erupt into conflict needing speedy adult intervention. At this age children play next to but not with each other. This is called "parallel play," playing alone in the presence of others. Nevertheless children benefit from the experience of being with other children. They are slowly beginning to learn social cooperation.

The Right Toy
At The Right Time:
SERIES *10*

NEST AND BUILD BLOCKS ™

At two-plus, the child is ready to undertake the challenge presented by this exciting set of nesting, variously shaped and sized building blocks.

The largest building block of all is the container itself. Lift off its cover and inside, neatly fitting, each inside the other, are rectangles, triangles and cylinders in varying sizes. Each block shaped is also a container which can hold the other smaller elements.

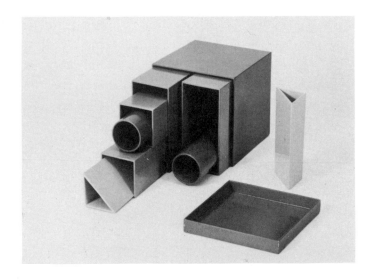

Simple or more complex structures can be built on the floor or table top. Returning the blocks to their container is a demanding and fascinating task that requires skills different from those used in building. This toy uses categorization by size, shape, volume and color on a more complex level. It can be used in as many ways as the child's imagination can devise, insuring it a long life as an increasingly versatile construction toy.

PICK AND PLAY
OBJECT
PUZZLES _™

Each puzzle panel has its own theme:
city life, transportation, and the home.
All three themes are designed to stimulate the child to identify the puzzle elements and to discover what is happening
in the scene: "There's the policeman.
What is he doing?" "Look—that's a tow
truck."

The puzzle elements are small, removable, three-dimensional pieces. Tak-
en out, they leave recesses in the panels
into which they can be replaced. The

puzzles, then, are form boards, but complex and interesting ones. Separated from the puzzle bases, the pieces become small toys to be played with in relation to the panel or along with blocks and other toys. *Pick and Play Object Puzzles* develop coordination between hand and eye, make a child more aware of the world around him, develop his understanding of categories of things that go together and in addition, are just plain fun!

The Part You Play: SERIES 10

Over and over again in this section which deals with parent roles, we have emphasized the importance of proceeding on the basis of your understanding of your own child and his capacities and needs. We might suggest that you give your child the *Nest and Build* blocks in the container and wait to see what happens, but for some children that would be a poor approach. Does your child especially like surprises? Does your child feel personal satisfaction in dealing with a mystery? Or does he become frustrated easily? There is no one right way of introducing this toy. We suggest that you do what seems the most fun for your youngster. Join in by all means if you wish and if he will enjoy it—but don't feel obliged to. Manipulate the parts—the rectangles can be flopped over, the cylinders can be rolled, the triangles can be examined in various ways. Join in building a boat, an apartment house, a barn if your child seems to relish sharing his play. But let the child lead in it. Be content to work within the child's own terms. If it seems right, help in putting the smaller into the larger containers. But be careful not to make it into a "must do" task.

These skills with be learned when the child is ready and then will be enjoyed. If for a while the shapes go back helter-skelter or don't seem to fit into the container at all, don't show the child that you can do it better. The point is for him to learn gradually to master the task, not for him to learn that a grown up will do it for him.

The *Pick and Play Object Puzzles* offer opportunities for communication between you and your child. Here are scenes and subjects to talk about. Examine them together: answer questions your child asks or tell about things that are pointed to—"That's a school bus. It takes children to school." "That's a policeman. He makes cars stop so we can cross the street." Relate the home scene to your child's home: "Does Daddy sit in a chair like that?" Help your child learn about the world, its places and things. "Which things have wheels?" "Which animal goes *moo?*" But most of all, let your child know that you enjoy being with him or her, talking and doing things together.

Growth Objectives: MONTHS 30 to 33

It is important to remember what was said at the beginning of the third year section. Your child at two is an individual—at two-and-half, often a volatile, moody individual, laughing one moment, crying the next—shifting from one extreme to the other—sunny and cooperative at eleven o'clock, angry and negative at twelve.

This is often a difficult period for the parent. It may be useful to realize that it is equally difficult for the child: Jimmy can't make up his mind—neither can Sally—every course of action is a two-way street and impulses pull both ways at once. This makes for obstinacy and unreasonableness. But there is a physical reason. The child of this age is less able to stop an action than to begin one. An object is grasped strongly but can only be let go of by flinging it away. There is sometimes difficulty in going to sleep—yet once asleep, difficulty in waking up. Characteristically, whatever the child does, he uses maximum strength or more strength than the task requires. Any change creates a problem. There is insistence that everything be done a certain way: a certain chair must always be used—a certain plate, spoon, and no other. Choices are so terribly difficult to make that certainties are clung to. Fortunately this is a transitional stage, lasting not too long a time. Soon, sensible choices will be arrived at. In a short time muscles will operate more smoothly. The child will be better able to stop an action, to unclench the hand, to set something down gently instead of flinging it violently away.

But now assertions of total independence compete with cries for total help, and dressing and undressing are apt to be problems. Some children resent clothes and pull them off as soon as they are put on. More often children make dressing into a game, running away from the harassed mother, delighting in being chased until she is exhausted and exasperated. Forcible dressing results in violent reaction. The child will be calmer when the mother is casual and able to wait or turn her attention to something else as if she did not care much one way or the other, about such things.

Language continues to develop. Children are genuinely interested in naming objects they know, particularly parts of the body. Try using this fact with your child. Try saying, "This is your foot," for instance, and then pop the sock on. Children are delighted with new or strange-sounding words, and do a good deal of chanting, stringing together new words and nonsense syllables. Dramatic play is well under way—children talk to their dolls or teddy bears and often, in their make-believe world, treat them with violence. The long-suffering toy may be soundly thrashed several times a day while lectured in a punishing voice.

The Right Toy
At The Right Time:
SERIES *11*

SO-BIG ACTION
PUZZLE _{TM}

Here is a giant, heavy cardboard, floor puzzle, a teddy bear at least as big as your child. The pieces fit together easily and the form is simple to build. It will not seem at all difficult to you, but for a small child, any fitting together is a challenge.

There is learning here of form, size, and space as well as the kind of activity

your independent, extra-active two-and-a-half-year old needs. When the bear is put together, the joints are made so that the arms and legs move. Small internal parts of the puzzle, like the bear's tie, can be picked out and replaced. In fact the largest puzzle piece contains a smaller form board type of puzzle.

Even when the child has learned how to put the bear together easily, the fact of having "a bear the size of me" will give pleasure. Later, when more complex toys demanding more advanced skills absorb your child's attention, the bear can be fastened together and used as a friendly wall decoration.

THE WONDER OF
GROWING
LIBRARY
AND RECORD

This beginner's library of eight books and a record take the child a step beyond the *Color Look Books.* The ideas are more complex and the language more varied.

Besides a charming ABC book and a counting rhyme book that teaches number concepts at the simplest level, there is a book that tells about how wild animals live and another that tells about farm animals. Then there are four real storybooks. The child is introduced to the characters. Things happen to these

story characters and they react. The stories have beginnings, middles and ends.

One story deals with the exciting idea of a nursery school and tells what nursery school children do. Then there is a warm story about family life. The familiar and the less familiar, reality and fantasy, are all here. Learning is here. Information about the real world—cities, farms, home, jungle, as well as the world of fantasy.

The record included with this library offers action songs for the active child. Songs that ask to be acted out in all kinds of ways: "Eensy-Weensy Spider"—fingers have to wiggle, "Everybody Do This"—hands have to clap and feet have to stamp—but most important, the child must listen and follow directions.

The Part You Play: SERIES *11*

At the half-year mark, as was pointed out in growth objectives, most children have a drive for independence and want to show that they can do things all by themselves. As a beginner at puzzle-solving, your child will probably need a little help to avoid frustration. There are many "No's" and "Let me, I can do it's." But the tactful parent will help the child put the puzzle together the first few times, seemingly just for the fun of doing it rather than to show how it is done. Conversation like, "Let me see, where would this piece go? Do you think it fits here?" helps the child to feel like a partner in the effort. Soon your child will learn to assemble the puzzle without any help, and the large size of the completed bear, constructed all by himself, will strengthen his feeling of competence.

The puzzle is constructed of heavy gauge cardboard, strong enough to survive the hard treatment you can be sure it will get.

The most satisfying feature of *The Wonder of Growing Library* is the opportunity it offers you and your child to be close as you read the stories aloud. Now the child is reaching out needing to relate to those most cared about. This new and deeper need to love as well as to be loved, expresses itself in many ways. One good way are the moments of pleasure in each other's company. Invite your child to snuggle close, look at the pictures together, enjoy those peaceful moments. Read the words, talk about the characters, guess what is going to happen, examine small details in the pictures. Relate the words and pictures, when they fit, to the child's life and to familiar circumstances.

These stories may be your child's first understanding of the sequence of events—the beginning, middle and end aspect of stories—and there is often sequence of an important kind in real life. Talk about this too. But most of all, create the feeling of something shared.

The record that accompanies the library of books has a record sleeve which illustrates the directions—ideas and actions that you can demonstrate. If the child has a simple record player, you can teach its use. These musical activities will be much more fun if you do them too, at least the first few times. You can help your child find the proper rhythm and timing and you can demonstrate the hand and body movements which go with the songs. Get Dad, or other members of the family, in on the action. Your child's delight in the music and his growing understanding of the songs is something the whole family can enjoy.

These songs are helping your child learn how to listen and follow directions. If the directions are not followed exactly, do not be concerned. The important thing is active involvement.

Growth Objectives: MONTHS 33 to 36

Reaching towards the three-year mark, the child is, typically, at a happy moment in development. The volatile, assertive, often violent two-and-a-half-year old is suddenly more serene, orderly, cooperative —anxious to behave as parents wish, and very proud to be doing so. There is, as well, a high degree of self-control. This lovely period will not last. But while it does, life is remarkably easy and enjoyable for the whole family.

The child's motor abilities have progressed. The feet are sure; the arms swing like an adult's when walking instead of being held away from the body for extra balance; the posture is erect. Sharp corners are turned without tipping over. Feet alternate on stairs. The pedals of the tricycle go round and round. "Just look at him go!"

Now the child can handle a spoon without tipping out its contents and can pour from a pitcher without spilling (if it is not too large or heavy or too full). The eye and hand are better controlled. Most children like to draw with large crayons and can become quite absorbed with projects.

This is the time when children become aware of three things. Some children may be able to count all the way up to three on fingers or toes, build a tower three blocks high, or notice three objects in a picture at one time—something which seems very simple, yet represents a great step forward. They are familiar with the three basic forms of circle, square and triangle. Keen observation is possible, and there is awareness and enjoyment working with different kinds of materials. Dramatic play is more developed and is characteristic of this age.

Language ability bounds forward. Now the child is capable of following language rules: putting s on plural words or ed on verbs when talking about the past. This is the time when, following the rules, children make errors that amuse the grown-ups. "The sheeps are in the field," or "Whobody is coming?" But these are positive mistakes for they show that rules are being applied. Reasoning is beginning and language is no longer just imitation. For adults do not say "sheeps" and "whobody." Now the child is truly beginning to be a language user, gaining power to say what he wants to say in his own way. He loves being read to, and begins asking questions about a set of happenings and learning from discussion.

Although still far from truly social, the child is much more conscious now of the feelings and wishes of others—and far more responsive to them. At times he is genuinely helpful, putting things away efficiently, picking up clothes, running simple errands. Now violence in play with another child does not occur as often, or burst forth unpredictably, and two children of this age may play well together for twenty minutes to a half hour—no small achievement.

Imaginative life is developing. Many children at this time like to pretend they are animals, imitating characteristic sounds and movements, wishing to be treated by the adults in the family as a dog, a rabbit, a cat—whatever has struck their fancy. This is all quite normal and is a way of coming to understand more about the world in which the child finds himself. This is also the period when many children have imaginary friends. If your child has an invisible companion, it is important to include the friend in activities when it is announced that he or she is along. Children's fantasies of this kind are a way of trying out their own identities to be sure of who they actually are. They learn from their imaginings, and from the degree of respect with which their elders treat their ideas.

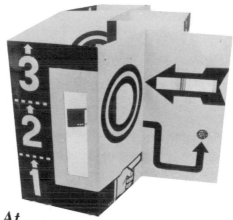

The Right Toy At The Right Time: SERIES *12*

THE PLAY CENTER ™

Here is a house, a tunnel, fort, store, school, puppet theatre or any structure your imaginative two-to-six year old child imagines it to be. It provides the strong sturdy prop for dramatic play. It can be sat in, crawled through, peeked into, peeked out of; built one way—moved—built another way. It is light enough to be set up and organized by the child, arranged in a wide variety of positions, opened as big as the play space allows, folded up easily and put away without taking too much room. It is the perfect toy for the time when small children reach out for friends and begin truly to want to do things with other

children. It can contain a group, fascinating and challenging its members to real group play. It is the ideal setting for Nina to entertain her dolls at a tea party, or for Joey to garage his cars or tricycle. It is useful both as a social experience playing with other children, or as a haven for solitary play.

The *Play Center* with its gay, bright graphics is just what its name implies: a focal point that stimulates many kinds of play—physical, imaginative, dramatic, noisy and energetic, quiet and domestic. It is background for whatever make-believe experiences your child's personality and age requires.

The Part You Play: SERIES *12*

This is a completely safe toy. Your child can lift it, set it up, open it, rearrange it, fold it. You can introduce it when your child is entertaining a friend or friends or on a rainy day when your child is alone and boredom is about to set in. When you first open the package help the child explore its possibilities. Help your child move the panels about, creating tunnels, rooms, a corridor or a maze. Make suggestions, or be enthusiastic about suggestions your child makes. If it is serving as a house, pretend to visit the lady of the house; if it is serving as a store, become a customer; if it is serving as a garage, drive in for gas or some interesting motor adjustment. You will be surprised as to the versatility of the *Play Center* and the information your child has learned, revealed as he plays different roles in this imaginative setting.

EPILOGUE

We hope that this book has helped you gain a deeper understanding of your child's mind and temperament, likes and dislikes, strengths and limitations. As you watch your three-year-old devising fresh ways of playing with the toys which have become tools of discovery; as you sense the reaching out towards new perceptions and skills as yet beyond your child's developmental level, we hope you will feel better equipped to help—to work with your child or at times to stand back and watch as he struggles and searches on his own.

If this book and toys have accomplished their purpose, they will have enhanced and helped to develop your own instinctive feelings as to the best way to support your child in learning and exploring, in growth and discovery. For the program was created to be an effective learning tool not only for your child, but for you as well.

After the third year, your child moves into a world that includes more pictures, more words, more categories of greater complexity. There will be questions—"What is this?, Why is that?"—reflecting a deeper need to know more about the world of reality and the world of imagination. Finer muscle coordination will be used, greater structures will be built, deeper social relationships will be possible.

After these first toys, described in this book, there

will need to be toys, materials, and experiences to match this new level of maturity. Each added month makes new demands upon you as parent—guide to the world. Remember—continue to observe sensitively, to listen thoughtfully, to accept your child's way of doing things with sympathic interest. Parents who act in these ways have the right to ask their children to accommodate themselves to the adult world, when it is necessary.

Love your child, give careful thought to natural progress, be available when needed, but never impede that aspect of his or her nature that demands launching out without your support. The sensitive balance between dependence and independence must be maintained and responded to by each of the important adults in the young child's life.

The world and all its ways is becoming your child's learning program, but for some years to come your love and interest, interpretation and help are vitally significant. You, as a parent, have the great good fortune of being the foundation stone and springboard for a new human being.

DR. ESTHER P. EDWARDS

MEMORIAM

ESTHER PASTENE EDWARDS died in a car accident April 19, 1971; now we, her friends, grieve that she is gone, yet rejoice that she has lived. She reached many people, somehow managing to bring her own belief to life—"there's something in the heart of everyone that responds to goodness."

Her education and experience reflect the myriad facets of a life dedicated to caring for people and ideas. Wellesley, Child-Walker School of Art, Boston University, Nursery Training School of Boston, and Harvard provided structure and stimulation for study. But she never did anything singly or simply. As she studied she worked—counselor, group worker, Headmistress, director of migrant child care centers, consultant, lecturer, author, inventor, teacher of children, professor at Tufts University.

She was a facilitating personality who gave unstintingly to others; she lived with zest and a loving concern; she knew young children well, and was dedicated to fostering education. Her stated beliefs about children permeated all her personal relations, "We cannot wipe out conflict and error in the young. We can only try to be there to help each child at the right moment to handle it. Our job is to teach children that all feeling is all right, but its expression needs channeling and control. To operate in such a setting makes great demands on the adult. It can only be done when there is a disinterested love for the child: a love which puts the child's growth above the adult's convenience. To teach from love is to be long-suffering and tolerant, but to stand fast when the issue warrants it demands all the maturity we can muster."

Thus Esther expressed her wisdom, her maturity, and her love. We have all been enriched and altered through our associations with her.

Evelyn Goodenough Pitcher, PH.D.
Eliot-Pearson Department of Child Study
Tufts University
Medford, Massachusetts

May 13, 1971